Dr. Mary Haase

780 - 475-9712

D1443202

The Ray of Hope

A Teenager's Fight Against
Obsessive Compulsive Disorder

The Ray of Hope

A Teenager's Fight Against Obsessive Compulsive Disorder

Ray St. John

Vermilion Press -2011

Vermilion Press

8008 E. 2600 N. Rd
Manville, IL 61319
Vermilionpress@gmail.com

Design and photographs by: H. Tak Cheung

The Ray of Hope: A Teenager's Fight Against Obsessive Compulsive Disorder/Ray St. John; forward by Joni St. John

ISBN 978-0-578-07032-2

First Printing, January 2011

Printed in China

In loving memory of

Grandpa

Robert Lee St. John

CONTENTS

FORWARD

This book is about obsessive compulsive disorder (OCD). Specifically, it is about one teenager's dealings with OCD. My son, Ray, has OCD that centers mainly on sexual matters. Why his OCD manifests itself this way, we have never figured out.

Many times I tried to get Ray to read about OCD. I gave him many, different books to read, even bribed him to read them. He would start out, but inevitably he would stop. I even tried to read some of these books to him, but to no avail. "Too boring," he would say of these books, or "I don't have time to read these books with all my homework." I also discovered that reading about others who have OCD would often trigger his own symptoms, a situation he found too uncomfortable. So with this experience in mind, Ray decided to arrange this book in a simple question and answer form. This way, readers can skip to those parts they most want to read and hopefully, won't be too bored.

There are times in this book where Ray repeats certain ideas. He did this because he knew that his readers would most likely skip around and not read through from beginning to end. After all, this is the way he would go through a book like this. It is his hope that the important ideas on OCD, at least from his perspective, are adequately emphasized in enough places so that all readers will easily find them.

Ray wrote this book to help teenagers who have OCD deal with it, especially those who have obsessions that are of a sexual nature. Having OCD is bad enough, but to have a type that is centered on such a sensitive issue as sex is even worse. He has tried to address OCD from as many aspects as possible, realizing that his readers are at different points in their OCD. Some may have yet to tell anyone about their "thoughts," some may have already openly talked about their OCD, but are not sure what to do, and yet others, may already have started treatment. Ray hopes that all comers to this book will find help and inspiration.

A word of caution to some readers: At times you might not be comfortable with what Ray has written. His obsessions are sexual, and many times he had to directly face this issue, and he had to face it often. You will see as you read how he did this. We both would like to apologize in advance to those who may find a few parts of this book uncomfortable. It was never the intention to offend or embarrass anyone.

I would encourage anyone who has OCD to learn as much about it as they can. There are many sources out there on OCD. There are books written by professionals who deal with OCD and memoirs by those who have a story to tell about their OCD. There are websites dedicated to those who have OCD; there is even an OCD foundation that addresses the many issues of this disorder. To help Ray deal with his OCD, I read and read and then read some more. No one book or source had everything we needed, but each one gave me something. I then added my own ingredients to the mix, and with time and a lot of patience, we finally accomplished what we set out to do: beat OCD.

What Ray has written is his own story. Some parts will be familiar to others who have OCD, whereas other parts will be strange. How OCD manifests and how it's treated varies with each affected individual. In a way, it's like a fingerprint. Each of us has similarities with others, but we also have our unique components. This variability in OCD makes it hard to understand, explain, study, and treat. I would encourage those readers who have OCD to consider writing their own stories. Tell the rest of us what it's like for you, what worked for you, who helped you the most, what books you read, and what mistakes you made. Even though your story is unique, I can guarantee that some fellow OCDer can benefit from your experiences.

OCD is an ugly disorder; it tries to rob all who have it from living a secure and thoughtful life. Many times, I watched Ray's OCD take him to dark places, places I feared that one day he could never return. But, he didn't let that happen. He fought his OCD with every weapon we could find. Some days he beat his OCD back, but on others he lost. If there is one message that the both of us would like to give others who have OCD, it is this: Don't ever give up. OCD can be beat.

Joni St. John, editor and mother

My OCD Story

My name is Ray, and I'm a teenager who has obsessive compulsive disorder (OCD). I am close to graduating from high school and am looking forward to college or wherever life happens to take me. My lifestyle now resembles that of a normal teenager: going out with friends and living an overall happy life. However, I lost several years of my life to OCD, and I came close to crashing and burning. There were many times when I wondered if I would ever get very far. In many ways, OCD has tried to stop me and take away my future, but I didn't let it. I beat it back.

My OCD first sparked to life when I was about five years old. I don't remember, but my mother tells me that for several weeks I constantly washed my hands. I would run into the bathroom and wash my hands several times within an hour. No one thought much about it at the time; they thought that I was just a little kid who had a temporary fascination with water. The OCD in me quieted down and remained so until I was about eight years old. At that time, I started asking questions about dying and if everyone around me was going to be all right. I would ask my mother strange questions like: Will everything be OK because I just touched the wall in my bedroom? I also remember that I would check, recheck, then recheck again to see if anything had fallen off my bed before I could sleep at night. I had no idea why I had these thoughts and to keep myself from worrying, I constantly asked my mother for reassurance. She readily gave it because she saw how anxious I was and because we had yet to understand that my thoughts were from OCD. As anyone who has OCD knows, giving reassurance doesn't help but only serves to feed the OCD. I got so bad that instead of just asking for my mom's reassurance about something, I would ask her to guarantee me that nothing bad would happen. Then, I asked her to super-guarantee me, next I asked for a super-super-guarantee, and finally, a super-super-super-guarantee.

My OCD quieted down again and remained so until I was about eleven years old. When it returned this time, it was when my family and I had just returned home from living a year in China. My father is Chinese, and he wanted me to spend some time with my grandmother, who lived in Shanghai. His job at a university allowed him to take a sabbatical leave, and he decided to work in Shanghai for a year. At the time, my mother was a pediatrician, and she decided to spend her time working at a children's hospital. I was sent to a Chinese middle school, where I was the only foreigner in the entire school and where no one spoke English. The idea was for me to learn to speak Mandarin (the official language of China), and I did pretty well. Even though we had all enjoyed our time in China, we were looking forward to coming home and restarting our lives in the U.S. The plans were for me to start sixth grade, for my mother to return to her pediatric practice in a small, rural area, and for my father to return to his university. At least these were our plans until OCD showed up again.

When OCD returned for the third time, it was more than just a little spark that would die out in a couple of weeks. This time, it quickly grew into a full-fledged fire that raged out of control. My symptoms had also changed this time. Instead of worrying about something bad happening, my obsessions took on a sexual nature. I obsessed over many, different aspects about sex. Was I a bad person because sexual images popped into my head? Did I accidently hurt someone in a sexual way without remembering that I had done it? Did I try to purposely bump into someone at a store because I secretly wanted to touch them in a sexual way? My mother also remembers times when I asked her strange questions like: How did she know for sure that I hadn't given her some kind of drug to knock her out and then sexually touch her? Or, how did she know for sure that someone hadn't just walked out of the woods, which is close to where we live, and that I hadn't molested them? And, true to OCD, I didn't just ask these weird questions a couple of times a day, I asked them constantly. I followed my mother around and incessantly begged her for reassurance that I hadn't done anything sexual that would have hurt someone. It got so bad for me that I started spending hours crying and wondering why this had happened to me. My mother remembers watching me curled up on a couch and crying like my heart was breaking. Nothing she did could stop my obsessions. No amount of reassuring me, distracting me with fun activities, or explaining to me that I was a good person could break the hold that OCD had on me. My mother realized that something serious was happening to me. What to do about it, however, wasn't clear to her at the time. She started thinking about what she would tell the parents of a pediatric patient who was having similar symptoms. She realized that one of the first things she would advise the parents to do was to decrease the stress in their home. And, that's what she did for me. She knew that if she returned to her practice in a small hospital that the stress level in our home would remain high. The constant pages and phone calls and the multiple evenings that she would need to return to the hospital would have taken their toll. She also knew that she wouldn't have the necessary time to help me. After considering all the factors, she decided not to return to medicine until the time she felt certain that I had recovered. This wasn't an easy decision for her. She had to give up a good part of her life to help me - career, financial independence, and the knowledge that she was helping people.

Amazingly, decreasing the stress level in our home worked. My obsessions quickly waned; I stopped crying for hours at a time; I decreased the number of times a day I hounded my mother for reassurance; and I generally, assumed a more normal life. My OCD, however, wasn't completely gone. It would spark on occasions, and my sexual obsessions would return. During these times, I would call out "bad thought," which was my way of asking my mother for reassurance. But, for the most part, I went about my life and acted like any other preteen. In fact, there were even times when my sexual obsessions were so quiet that I masturbated as frequently as any of my friends. I could laugh at sexual jokes, watch sexual scenes on TV, and look at girls as easily as anyone my age.

Once we recognized that my problems came from OCD, my mother started reading books on it. Even though she was a pediatrician, she didn't have any expertise in treating mental disorders like OCD. She had been trained to diagnose mental disorders and treat the milder ones, but not the ones that were more difficult and involved. The knowledge she gained through her reading helped her to understand that we weren't alone, that many others have this condition, that sexual obsessions are fairly common (especially in males), and that there are professionals who can help us. She even used ideas from the OCD books, like naming my OCD so that we could separate the OCD from my other, more normal thoughts. Armed with our new knowledge on OCD, we felt confident that if OCD struck me again that we could handle it. We were wrong, so very wrong.

The first hints that my OCD was coming back started during the summer before I started high school. As my sexual obsessions slowly returned, we tried what we had learned to get rid of them. But, nothing worked. Instead of getting better and going on, my obsessions grew and multiplied. Every day, something new would trigger my obsessions. Eventually, I got so that I couldn't go anywhere, couldn't watch most TV programs, or couldn't talk with my friends without feeling extreme anxiety. My mother hated going to movies with me because I had to tap her shoulder and say "bad thought" multiple times during the movie. I couldn't even get through the Harry Potter movies without having problems. It was like my world was gradually closing in around me. There were only a few places where I felt safe and even those were becoming bothersome to me. Many times, I didn't even need an external trigger to set me off, my own mind formed sexual thoughts or images on its own. There was nowhere I could go to get away from my OCD. It was everywhere.

I started my freshmen year in high school at the same time my OCD was gaining momentum. My mother fought it every step, but there finally came a time when she decided that we needed help. By this time, I feared every imaginable aspect of sex and would go to extremes to avoid feeling bad. The worst part for me was when I started obsessing about my own bodily secretions, namely semen. I would check often to assure that no semen had leaked out and would undergo extreme washing if I thought that even a drop had been secreted. As my OCD progressed, I even started worrying about how semen could possibly have been transmitted throughout my house. For some reason, I started focusing on a certain bathroom that I had often used when I was still "normal" and had no problems masturbating. My OCD mind convinced me that semen was still present in that bathroom, which was subsequently renamed the "evil bathroom" by my mother, even though I had long given up masturbation. I considered anything or anybody that went into that bathroom as contaminated and probable carriers of the dreaded substance. Wherever they went and whatever they touched was also considered contaminated. Even objects several degrees removed from the original carrier were not safe in my mind. There were so many dirty objects and places in my house that I couldn't keep track of them. Eventually, it just got easier to consider the whole house as unclean and unsafe.

When I was at my worst, I was close to giving up on life. I was still going to school, but barely. I hadn't met with my friends for several months, and my family relationships were quickly deteriorating. I can't remember everything that I was doing during that time, but my mother does. Here is some of what she remembers.

- I washed my hands so much that they became red, chapped, and often bled.
- I started washing my arms up to my elbows because washing just my hands didn't make me comfortable anymore.
- I started washing my feet because I was worried that the floor had somehow gotten contaminated by semen. I did this by splashing water on the bottom of my feet several times each day. By the evening, the rug by the sink was drenched and would drip water if picked up.
- I took up to four showers a day because I felt dirty every time I had a sexual obsession, and because I was never sure whether or not I had touched any semen.
- I insisted that my mother wash my clothes even when they were clean. She remembers that there times when I had my hand on a

pile of shirts, had an obsession, and then insist that the entire pile be washed before I would wear any of them.

- I insisted that my mother wash all of my bedding whenever I thought I had leaked any semen during sleeping.

- I couldn't walk across any floors in our house without having anxiety because I was convinced that many areas of the floor were dirty. I would jump from place to place to get where I wanted, which was usually the sink so that I could wash my hands, arms, elbows, and feet.

- I couldn't touch any doorknobs in our house without using a napkin or piece of paper as a barrier. I was convinced that all doorknobs weren't safe for me to touch.

- I couldn't touch any car doors for the same reasons I couldn't touch doorknobs.

- I wouldn't use any eating utensils my mother placed on the table because I thought that her hands weren't clean enough, and I would get others from the drawer.

- I wouldn't eat anything that I thought my mother had touched with her hands. If I even suspected that she had touched some food, I refused to eat it.

- I refused to let my mother touch me in any

way because I was sure she had been contaminated. She couldn't hug me, brush against me in any way, or hand me anything. She couldn't even stand close without me having problems.

To handle my OCD, I was evaluated by a psychiatrist, was put on medication, and spent several sessions talking with a psychologist. My OCD slowly improved for several months, but then I stalled. It was like I was stuck, no going forward but no slipping backward either. We changed medication, debated about returning to my psychologist, and thought about changing psychiatrists and/or psychologists. We did none of these things. Instead, my mother decided to try treating my OCD on our own. She worried that time was running out for me and that OCD would soon irreversibly affect my life. Her patience had also run out with the professionals; they didn't help me to the extent she thought I needed.

How did we treat my OCD? Were we successful? In this book, I explain how we handled the many, different aspects of dealing with OCD. It is my hope that what I have written will help those who are also affected by OCD. I realize that not all of what I tell will help everyone, but I hope that those who pick up this book will find at least one thing that they can use to help them fight back their OCD.

And yes, we were successful. OCD no longer has

a hold on my life.

In this book, I try to answer some of the many questions that come up when dealing with OCD. I used a simple question and answer format because I wanted to give my readers a quick way to find what is important to them and to allow them to skip over the other parts. I also used this format because it's the one that I find most useful. I have never been a patient reader, and I lose interest in a book when it's not quickly giving me what I want. I also wrote this book in a way that sounds like a conversation between me and those teenagers who also have OCD. I wanted this book to be personal and for my readers to feel like I'm close by and willing to help them get through this difficult time in their lives.

As my readers will quickly determine, my mother's role in helping me through my OCD was varied. Sometimes, she was my mother who held my hand and provided me with comfort, but at other times, she was my main therapist who created and then implemented my treatment plan. She also used her medical training to help guide me through many, difficult decisions regarding medications. Because of these different roles, I didn't feel as though it would be accurate to simply refer to her as my mother in this book. Instead, I decided to call her Dr. M (short for Dr. Mom).

WHY DID YOU WRITE THIS BOOK, AND WHY SHOULD I READ IT?

One reason that I wrote this book is because it serves as yet another victory over my OCD. Even though I had successfully defeated OCD, I knew that writing this book would bring up difficult memories and emotions. But, I also knew that I need to remember what I had been through so that when OCD tries to take over again (as it often does), I can keep the necessary skills for defeating OCD close at hand. For me, this book serves as a recap of my difficulties with OCD. Going over what I had suffered from in the past allows me to recognize those suffering points and to stop them in the future. By writing this book, I have solidified my abilities at recognizing OCD thoughts and at conducting self-therapy. I know these skills will adequately serve me through the rest of my life. In a way, this book has helped me as much as I hope reading it will help you. I now have a source that I can go back to and help me remember what I have done. In short, I have written my own guide to helping myself. I also wrote this book for myself in the sense that it helps me remember that I no longer have anything to be afraid of. And, if I do become afraid because of my OCD, I can acknowledge and master my worst fears.

Of course, I also wrote this book in hope of helping you, my readers, especially those of you who have sexual obsessions. To fully deal with this type of OCD, you need therapists and family members who are prepared to deal with sexual topics. I fear that many therapists and parents do not have the stoutness to do what it takes to defeat this type of OCD. To truly deal with sexual obsessions, you have to face many, different aspects of sexuality. For example, (for you males) as part of your treatment plan you may be encouraged to go into the bathroom and stimulate yourself into having an erection or to do other strange sexual exposures (more about this type of therapy later). At one point in my therapy, Dr. M and I spent hours looking at *Hustler* (a very explicit pornographic magazine). Believe me, these activities were very hard for me to do, but I got through them and amazingly, each time I did these things, my OCD seemed a little further away. But, I could only do this because Dr. M has absolutely no fear of discussing sexual topics and of facing this type of OCD. I hope that by openly discussing sexual issues in this book, it makes it easier and more comfortable for you and for those around you to face and defeat your sexual obsessions.

I also believe that you should read this book because I can answer some of the impossible questions you ask yourself. I know what you are going through. I can reassure you that your OCD is nothing more than a trick of your mind and that what you fear is not real. Many times, I wished I had others to talk to about my OCD. I wrote this book because I want you to know that you are far from being alone. Loneliness is the worst feeling in the world, especially when you doubt yourself and your worthiness. I think that this type of lonesomeness is one of the most severe forms of mental pain. I should know, I felt it for several years. I want to save you from this pain, and Dr. M and I know that we can if you read this book.

Why did OCD happen to me?

I don't know, and I doubt if anyone can really answer this question. I think that someday science will answer this but until then, we just have to accept, without knowing why, we have OCD. But, we are not alone. The best estimate is that OCD afflicts around two million people in the United States. About 1 in 200 kids have OCD, and about 1 in 40 adults have it. I think that most of us who have OCD fail to realize how common OCD is and think that we are alone in this struggle. I also suspect that the actual number of people who have OCD in the world is higher than what the experts state, because many of us who have OCD are quite good at hiding our symptoms. How would these OCDers ever get counted? For me, knowing that so many others were going through the same things that I was gave me strength. Once I understood that many others felt like me and had fought back their OCD, I was encouraged.

I have often felt (as I'm sure you do) how unfair it was that I had to deal with OCD. At times, I had also wondered if I had done something terribly wrong and that OCD was my punishment. Of course, this thinking is ridiculous. None of us did anything to deserve our OCD. It just happened; it was bad luck. We have OCD because the right combination of factors came together at the right time. No one yet knows just what all these factors are, but I know that in time, OCD will be better understood. Currently, the factors known to associate with OCD are not many but include such things as heredity (conditions that run in families), certain personality types (eg, highly sensitive), and certain environmental conditions (eg, intense family interactions).

My advice is not to spend too much time wondering why OCD happened to you. There are no clear answers. You need to use your time and energy in a much more important and productive area: fighting OCD back.

How has OCD affected your life?

OCD has affected my life in many ways and according to Dr. M, these affects were all negative. To her, OCD has no redeeming qualities whatsoever. Even though some OCDers can use their obsessions in advantageous ways, Dr. M. still doesn't accept the idea that having OCD is good. Some of us who have OCD, for example, have the type where we are perfectionists and can't stand the idea of making mistakes. Students with this type of OCD may redo their homework over and over again because they don't feel that it is quite right and will only turn it in when it appears perfect to them. A doctor who has this type of OCD may appear caring and thorough; no detail is too small to escape his (or her) attention. At first glance, this doctor appears quite good and one that takes great care of patients. But, there is a major difference between this doctor and other great doctors. The behavior of the OCD-affected doctor is directed mainly by fear. For these doctors (or anyone else who has this type of OCD) there is never any satisfaction of a job well done or pride in what they have accomplished. There is only the obsession of fear of what will happen next and how to avoid anything bad from happening.

Because my mind was trapped by my obsessions, I often did many stupid and counterproductive things.

Sometimes I washed items that were never meant to withstand water, let alone soap and lots of water. Looking back, I am astounded at the number of times I washed my homework because I felt it was contaminated. One would think that common sense and reason would have eventually stepped in and kept me from washing yet another piece of paper only to watch it disintegrate in the water. But, that is one of the hallmarks of OCD: The destruction of common sense. Dr. M also had to closely watch me to keep me from cleaning things like computer keyboards, cell phones, wallets, or ATM cards. Many of these things would not have done well had I been allowed to de-contaminate them when my OCD wanted me to.

Most times, I washed items that were mine, but I remember one time when my friend tossed his cell phone at me asking me to use it to call another friend about something (I've long forgotten what I was to ask). As his cell phone touched my hand, my OCD immediately began screaming at me that my hand was contaminated. I started agonizing over the remote possibility that semen had seeped through my pants and that it had somehow gotten onto my hand that I was using to hold the cell phone. My mind then jumped to the idea that the next time my friend used his cell phone, his mouth, ear, and hand would become contaminated by semen. The immediate guilt I felt by that possibility overwhelmed me to the extent I couldn't stand it. So, I ran to the nearest bathroom using the excuse that I wanted to go there to make the call (weird I know, but my friend didn't question me). Once in the bathroom, I lightly applied some soap and proceeded to wash the phone. Luckily for me, the phone didn't break.

My OCD also caused me to lose track of many things. Because of my irrational fear of semen and its power to cause havoc in my world, I couldn't put things in my pockets, especially those that are close to my genital area. Most teenagers keep a wallet or a cell phone in their pants pocket, but there was no way I could do this without feeling extreme anxiety. So, I often carried my wallet and cell phone in my well-washed, semen-free hand. But, I would obviously need to put these things down whenever I needed to do something else. As you can imagine, I often lost my wallet and cell phone because I would forget to pick them back up again. I spent a lot of time back-tracking to where I had been, trying to locate whatever it was I had lost yet again. Most times, I found my lost item, but sometimes, I couldn't and would have to tell Dr. M what I had lost. We would then start planning what to do about it and try to work on preventing such losses from happening again.

To keep me going and partially functional, Dr. M continuously patrolled those areas where I often spent time. She remembers constantly going through all our household wastebaskets looking for homework, important forms, wallet, cell phone (all the listed items had been thrown away at one time – many of them repeatedly), and anything else that was important to me. Almost every day, she pulled something out. But, of course, I refused to touch whatever it was and insist that it somehow be cleaned. This situation often caused a dilemma for Dr. M. Should she let the item be cleaned, which would enable my OCD and make it worse, or should she just leave the item where it was and let me suffer the consequences? Or, was there some middle ground she could take? She knew that doing well in school was as important to my future opportunities as was getting control of my OCD. So, depending on the importance of the item, the time of day, the intensity of my OCD at the moment, and her patience level, she would use different approaches. Sometimes, we would be successful, and I would move forward, but on other times, OCD would win. It took us endless time and energy to maneuver around these situations.

Many of my OCD-induced behaviors also adversely affected my relationships with those around me. I think that many people generally viewed me negatively because they only saw what I had done, but didn't understand why I had done it. Many times I heard my parents and teachers say things like: "Why can't you keep track of your things? Why should I let you borrow any of my things, you will only break or lose them. Why is it that you always need extra homework sheets? Why should I let you turn your homework in late again? Why didn't you hear me the first two times I told the class about the assignment?" I heard an endless number of these questions during the time when OCD had me down. At the time, I couldn't answer those around me, but could only act embarrassed and ask yet again for what it was I needed. Looking back, I wished I had the words to explain what OCD was doing to me. I wanted to let others know that I wasn't being rude, belligerent, or purposely trying to get away with something. It was just that my obsessions were often churning so fast in my brain that it was hard for any new information to break through. OCD also had me so blinded by fear that I had little awareness that what I was doing was causing others difficulty.

CAN YOU SEE ANY GOOD TO HAVING OCD?

I think that some good can come from having
OCD. Dr. M and I disagree on this; she says that she
hates OCD too much to ever think positively about
it in any way, and I can understand why she thinks
this way. She has watched OCD take so much from
me: friends, confidence, strength, and peace. And,
I think that I would feel the same way if I hadn't finally gotten my life back from OCD, but I did. I am
mentally healthy, and I can now look back at the road
that OCD has forced me to travel. Am I stronger
or a better person for having travelled that road? I
think so.

OCD has shaped the person I am today. The scars
OCD have left on me have made me one hundred percent different than I would be had I not had OCD. But,
the battle with OCD has also left me with some well-
learned lessons that have helped me progress further in
life than many of my peers. This said, however, I do
not think that having OCD is good or preferable, but
you must deal with the cards you are dealt.

Aristotle famously said, "We cannot learn without pain." If this is true, then I think that those of
us who have OCD and have defeated it, should be
awarded an honorary Ph.D. in life. I know that I
have learned a lot. I can now understand others easier, and I no longer make assumptions about people

without knowing all the necessary facts about them. I have learned not to fear those who behave strangely or appear out of the ordinary. After all, maybe their strangeness results from a mental illness like mine. I also have learned to ignore those who make fun of me for various reasons and who try to put me down. Why should I pay any attention to these people? They know nothing about me and nothing about what I have been through. I realize now that by feeling the pain of OCD, I can empathize with those who are also in pain. I don't judge them for what they fail to do, but admire them for trudging on.

Having OCD has also taught me to identify and to appreciate what is important in life. When I was at my worst with OCD, I felt as if I didn't want to live anymore. I think that when we brush that close to death, it changes us and our perspectives. I can see and feel things clearer now. Because of OCD, I have also seen and felt Dr. M's absolute and unconditional love. She never wavered in her love and never gave up on me. How many people in our lives can we truly say that about? I know that no matter what happens in my life that my "rock" will always be there for me to stand on. I also think that OCD has affected me in how I perceive my future. I came so close to losing parts of it that I now protect it much more closely. I think a lot about what I want to do and how I want to help others live a good life. I refuse to let events or people dictate to me who I should be and what I should do. I have fought hard for my future and will not easily give it up. OCD may wreck your life, but there is much that you can salvage from the wreckage and use to rebuild after you gather the right tools and the strength to move on.

Why do you think you have sexual obsessions instead of something else?

This is a question I have asked myself a lot. I have played with many different ideas but have never come up with anything definite. Perhaps, it was because I developed my worst OCD symptoms during a time when I was also experiencing puberty. Was it the surges in testosterone (the male hormone that is most involved in causing our sex drives) that my body was having that also affected my OCD? I don't know for sure. But, it is known that puberty and OCD are strongly associated and that more males than females who have OCD develop sexual obsessions. Other information on OCD also suggests that sex hormones are involved in OCD. New mothers, for example, who didn't have any previous problems with OCD, can sometimes develop it shortly after having a baby and some women whose ovaries have developed certain problems can also suddenly develop OCD.

Another idea I had about why some of us have sexual obsessions deals with the strong influence that sex has on our society. Sex is everywhere, and the messages we get about it are very confusing for those of us who are trying to grow up. In some situations, sex is good (and actually encouraged), but in others, it's considered taboo. Added to this mix is the way most adults shy away from talking about it. How are we supposed to get good guidance on this important part of our lives if it isn't openly talked about without embarrassment? Thinking and dealing with sexual issues causes anxiety in most teenagers. I think that for some of us this uncertainty and confusion actually contributes to our OCD.

I have decided that inquiring why I have sexual obsessions rather than checking obsessions or anything else is totally irrelevant. I know that if OCD hadn't approached me in the manner that it had, that it would have appeared in another form. Instead of worrying about sexual issues all the time, I could have just as easily been checking the door locks a thousand times a day or needing to count to a particular number every other minute of the day. The sexual obsessions of OCD did not happen to me because I have something wrong with my morality (or for any other reason); it just happened. I have realized that instead of wondering why I have a particular type of obsession, I need to view these obsessions as an enemy that has chosen me for no particular reason.

Am I an evil person because I have sexual obsessions?

No. I can say without any hesitation that you are not an evil person. But, I can understand why you might ask this question. I remember often wondering about my goodness. How could I be good if I was always having such bothersome thoughts? To deal with this, I used several different strategies to help me remember that I am a good person despite my seemingly perverse thoughts. Among these strategies include: 1) reminding myself that most, if not all, people have similar thoughts (the difference is they don't dwell on the thoughts), 2) reminding myself that I have never acted on these thoughts in any way, and 3) listing the good things that I have done. These three strategies have often worked for me and kept me convinced that I am not an evil person.

Always remember that OCD is a trickster. It tricks and torments you into thinking that you are evil because you have these strange thoughts. It never lets you be, and almost anything you see or experience causes your thoughts to start churning. After a while, you become so confused that you even question your inherent goodness and worth. My quest to becoming OCD free began when I recognized OCD for what it really is: a flaw in several of my brain pathways.

Before I understood what OCD was and how it

works in my brain, I had often worried that because I had such persistent sexual obsessions, it meant that I was some kind of sexual predator. I questioned my morality. How could I be considered good if my thoughts were this bad? And, if I am a good person, what's the difference between me and an actual sexual predator? Surprisingly, the answers to these questions are quite clear. I am good because I hate these thoughts. I am good because these thoughts scare me. Sexual predators, in contrast, find some kind of enjoyment in thinking their sexual thoughts. And, predators often act on their thoughts.

Another question I'm sure you have: How do you know that you will never act on these thoughts? Maybe you think that you really don't have OCD, but are actually someone who is destined to a life of crime. To answer this, look again at what OCD is and think again about how your thoughts make you feel. If you mainly receive pleasure or excitement from having these thoughts, then you don't have OCD. You do need help, just a different kind than what we OCDers need. If, however, you mainly feel disgust, fear, anxiety, or panic when you have your thoughts, then you definitely have OCD.

Yet another way to see your goodness: How far do you go to assure yourself that you don't cause anyone harm? I used to believe that my actions would cause harm to someone I didn't know and who was totally and irrevocably innocent. I used to believe that after accidently touching my pants, I would transfer semen to my hand, which then might infect others if I didn't immediately wash my hands. I didn't really know what this infection actually meant, but it somehow tied into morality. I believed that my actions would cause the desecration of the morality of some innocent child or adult. I know this sounds absurd, but these thoughts inflicted a substantial toll on me because I could not get absolute reassurance that I would not cause harm to anyone. To keep the world safe from me and the harm I thought I could cause, I went to extreme measures. I washed and washed, and then washed again my hands, arms, and feet (trying desperately to wash away all possibility of semen contamination). I was extremely vigilant about what I touched and how I touched it (eg, used papers to open doors or waited until someone else opened the door for me). I was even careful about where I walked on the floor at my home. Wasn't it possible that I had stepped on some semen in the bathroom and then walked all over the floor, which meant that it was now contaminated? The list of things I did to protect those around me was endless. If I were an evil person, would I have worried so much and used such extreme measures? I don't think so. My OCD thinking may have shattered my life, but I know, without a doubt, that I am a good person.

Am I a pervert for having sexual obsessions?

No, you are definitely not a pervert because you have sexual obsessions. You have OCD that just happened to take sexuality as its subject and not something else like germs, symmetry, or religion. How do I know this for sure? Simple: You are worried about it. If you were some kind of sexual predator or pedophile, then you wouldn't be worried about your thoughts. Instead of sending you into a panic every time a sexual obsession crossed your mind, you would actually find the thought pleasurable.

Another reason that I'm sure we're not perverts is because no one who has this type of OCD has been arrested for a sexual-based crime. The ranks of sexual predators and pedophiles are not filled with OCDers, but people who have other, more pathological problems. In other words, we don't hurt anyone. And, we go to extreme measures to assure ourselves that we never will. In my case, I washed my hands and feet to make sure that no one would become contaminated with semen; I repeatedly told Dr. M about my bad thoughts so she would know; and I made sure never to accidently bump into anyone. Are these behaviors of someone who is dangerous and should be locked away? Wouldn't a criminal who is looking to hurt someone, do the opposite of what

I was doing?

Many times, those of us who have a mental disorder worry unnecessarily about our morality. We watch the news and see people committing horrendous crimes. Every day we hear about murder and rape and sometimes, we even hear about how those crimes were committed by someone who has a mental illness. I have no doubt that many crimes result because of a mental disorder. But, it's never us OCDers who commit these crimes. The only people we ever hurt are ourselves and our families.

Can I still go to college even though I have OCD?

There is nothing you cannot do if you have OCD. This could also be said vice versa; you could also lose your entire life to OCD. To prevent this from happening, you must make all the necessary effort needed to defeat OCD. College can be scary, but if you know how to defeat OCD and to destroy any new OCD thoughts before they grasp a hold of you again, then college will work for you.

To get to college, however, you must first navigate through high school. I found that OCD and high school were a tough combination. Many times, OCD pushed me back in school. I found it hard to pay attention and because of that, some teachers didn't think much of me. I am now where I need letters of recommendation for college or for scholarships and am not in a good position to get them from some of my teachers. But, I won't let that stop me. If I quit trying now, then OCD wins, and I will never let that happen. I have come too far.

Dr. M has often said she wished she could write a letter of recommendation for me. Who better to know what I have been through? As a lark, she actually wrote one for me, and I couldn't resist sharing it with you.

Director of Admissions
Wonderful University
Somewhere, USA

Dear Dr. Wonderful,

I am writing this recommendation in support of Mr. Ray St. John. First, I would like to acknowledge the unusual nature of this letter. I am Ray's mother and have obviously, known Ray for a long time. I can tell you more about Ray and his struggles, accomplishments, and his strengths than anyone else.

No doubt you are accustomed to reading letters from teachers, coaches, employers, and other mentors. I am none of these to Ray, but I do have a perspective about Ray that no one else has, and I think that these parts of Ray are important for you to know.

Ray has obsessive compulsive disorder (OCD), a mental condition that is known by its recurring negative thoughts and compulsions, which are often performed to decrease the anxiety of these thoughts. Currently, the main treatment for OCD is called exposure and response prevention therapy (ERP). With this therapy, a person is exposed to that which they fear and are encouraged not to run from that fear. In other words, if one wants to improve their OCD symptoms, then they have to repeatedly face what they fear the most.

Ray has been successful in using ERP. Through several sessions, which were conducted during school breaks, he faced his most dreaded fears and in doing so, has dramatically improved his OCD. Through his diligence, hard work, and perseverance he has reduced his OCD symptoms to essentially nothing.

Throughout the time when Ray's OCD was active, Ray chose not to reveal his condition to anyone, such as teachers or coaches. It was his desire that he be viewed in the same way as everyone else. In other words, Ray never wanted anyone to think that he was using his disorder as an excuse. His grades and his accomplishments were achieved without any special accommodations for his OCD.

I am confident that you have received many applications from students that are filled with extracurricular activities, service projects, and job experiences. You will not see such an extensive list on Ray's application. His time and energy was needed to work on improving his OCD symptoms. Many times, Ray has expressed the wish that college applications had a clear place for accomplishments like his. Ray spent several Christmas vacations, spring breaks, and summer vacations dealing with his OCD. When other students were enjoying their breaks, Ray was working hard. We understood that if Ray was to preserve his future opportunities that he needed to defeat his OCD first. The efforts that this endeavor took were immense and left little time for Ray to participate in other activities.

Every university wants students who are hard working, diligent, persistent, creative, and responsible. I can assure you that Ray used every one of these characteristics to handle his OCD. No one could solve his OCD for him. It was solely up to Ray to take the necessary action and responsibility for *defeating his OCD. My role was only that of a coach or advisor.*

Ray freely admits that there are areas in his life where he currently falls short. His grades, even though good (all A's and B') are not up to the standard by which he now holds himself. He also realizes that he shows a lack of leadership and participation. He is currently striving to improve these areas and feels that he will soon catch up to his peers.

In my opinion, your university would greatly benefit from students like Ray. Students who have struggled to overcome an obstacle, such as OCD, often have more maturity and persistence than others. Furthermore, they have often developed the ability to empathize with others who are struggling in life.

I can truly say that there is no one I admire more than Ray. I have watched him struggle, grow, and then succeed. What he has accomplished in his short life is more than many of us ever will.

Sincerely,
Joni St. John, M.D.

I did all right in high school even though I had many tough times. I got A's and B's and managed to take most of the hard courses. There were times, however, when some teachers wanted to keep me down and not let me take some of the classes I wanted to. Because of OCD, I had struggled in some courses, which made several teachers think that I didn't have the ability to take some of the harder courses. There was even one time when I took a class on an override. In other words, a teacher didn't think I could do it. But, I knew I could. Dr. M backed me up, and off I went (by the way, I did OK – got a B). Another time when I couldn't get approval to take a course I wanted, I took an online course over the summer. After successfully completing the course, I was then allowed to go on. What I am trying to tell you here is that OCD will make school harder for you, but there are things you can do to make it work. First of all, accept any support your parents give you. Dr. M helped me keep track of homework, asked a lot of questions every day about school, kept close track of my grades, and always believed that I could be successful in whatever course I wanted to take. Of course, there were times when I found this extremely annoying; what teenage boy wants his mother looking over his shoulder all the time, but I know now that it helped me get through. Second, be prepared to have a plan b, and even a plan c, when the first one doesn't work out. OCD often derailed my plans for school, and I had to find alternate ways to get where I wanted. You might have to take extra classes at summer school or spend time explaining to teachers why you should be allowed to do what you want. All this takes time and effort, but my advice to you is to do it.

Even if OCD has completely messed up your high school experience and decreased your chances of getting into college, there are still ways you can get there. It just might take a little longer. If your ultimate goal is for a university degree, you could start out at a community college and work your way from there. You could also start slow and take only a few (or even just one) class at a time. OCD may slow you up a bit, but it won't stop you if you refuse to let it.

Will I pass my OCD on when I have kids?

Some of what causes OCD is genetic. This means that the same stuff (ie, DNA) that causes us to look like our parents or siblings can also contribute to us having OCD. It has been estimated that over 50% of the cause of OCD is from genetic factors. What this also means is that, in addition to our genes, there are other factors, such as our home environments, past histories of trauma, or how our parents chose to raise us, that also determines when and if OCD appears. In other words, if you have OCD, the chance that your child will also have OCD is higher than it is for someone who does not have OCD. At the same time, however, it is not a sure thing that you will pass on your OCD.

Exactly how OCD is passed on has yet to be determined, but I think that researchers will soon have some more answers. To help them out, Dr. M and I joined a study that was looking at the OCD-genetic connection. We spent several hours on the phone answering questions about our symptoms and histories, filled out several pages of forms, and even had our blood drawn. Even though we had beaten back OCD, we wanted to help those who are studying OCD to find out just exactly how it is passed between generations. We hope that once researchers have that answer, then a medication that specifically targets OCD can be developed.

Once Dr. M and I understood what OCD was and how it can present, we realized that I was not the sole OCDer in our family. Shortly after my OCD presented itself, Dr. M realized that her mother, my maternal grandma, also had signs of OCD. The most identifiable symptom of hers was the time when she obsessed about how my grandpa might get struck by lightning. Her compulsions consisted of constantly following him around to make sure he was all right or constantly looking at the sky to see if there were any storms approaching. Dr. M remembers that shortly after I was born, her mother came to stay with us to help out. During that time, she would often run to the window to see what the weather was doing. It never occurred to her OCD brain that she was in a different county than where my grandpa was and that the weather was most likely different in the two places.

After Dr. M realized that her mother most likely had OCD (my grandma died about one year after I was born so it isn't possible to really know for sure), she began to take a closer look at her own ways of thinking and behavior. She wondered if she had OCD but had somehow found ways to keep it at bay and not let it stop her. Dr. M's conclusion: She also has OCD; it just looks different from mine. Instead of having sexual-based obsessions, she obsesses over inadvertently causing harm to others and her compulsions consist mainly of checking and rechecking to make certain that she has not hurt anyone. I always thought that this was an interesting obsession for a pediatrician to have. The triggers for these types of obsessions are everywhere in a doctor's office. All the patients she had to see every day, all the phone calls she had to deal with, and all the baby deliveries she had to attend were a constant source of anxiety for her. In retrospect, Dr. M realizes that her constant worry about taking good care of her patients was not only because she was conscientious (she definitely was), it was also because of OCD. One time I asked Dr. M if having OCD helped her become a better doctor. She quickly reminded me that having OCD is never a good thing and that if one wants to be good at something, there are much more productive and healthy ways to get there than by having a mental illness.

Presently, Dr. M is fine and has no OCD symptoms. She says this is partly because she no longer practices medicine and is not constantly exposed to what bothers her. She also thinks that by helping me through my OCD problems, she has learned to keep her own symptoms at bay. Not long ago, for example, she was involved in a flu clinic where she had to inject people with a vaccination. A couple of days afterward, she started obsessing about whether or not she had hurt someone. Did she measure the vaccinations right? Did she use the right markings on the syringes? Will someone get sick or even die because she didn't give their vaccination correctly? She started checking everything she could so that she could feel better and reassure herself that she had done everything right. Then, it hit her. This thinking was not right; it was her OCD trying to flare up. Once this realization occurred to her, she quickly fought back, and her OCD disappeared.

Should the possibility of you passing on your OCD keep you from having children? Definitely not. Making the decision that you are not going to have children will limit your possibilities in life and may decrease your happiness. Also, there is no one better prepared than you to deal with your child's OCD should it appear. Because of your experience, you will know what symptoms to look for and how to stop your child's obsessions at their first onset. If you work hard now and learn all there is to know about OCD and how to defeat it, then you will be well prepared to deal with any future occurrence of OCD.

Many of us who have OCD show minor symptoms when we are very young. Our parents, Dr. M included, often fail to recognize those symptoms and dismiss them as nothing more than a child's imagination. These early OCD symptoms also often fade away without any intervention. The first time Dr. M remembers any symptoms even remotely resembling OCD was when I was about five. For about a week, I repeatedly ran into the bathroom to wash my hands. She didn't know what to think about my hand washing and just when she was getting more concerned, I stopped. My OCD remained quiet until I was about eight, which was the time when I started obsessing again. I would ask Dr. M repeatedly if everything was all right and if something bad was going to happen. I strangely worried that if I touched certain objects that somehow my touching them would cause something terrible to happen. I did this for about one month and had progressed to the point that I wanted Dr. M to guarantee me, then super-guarantee me, then super-super-guarantee me that nothing bad would happen. She continually reassured me and again, the symptoms disappeared.

What Dr. M wishes she had known during my early symptoms of OCD was that these thoughts were indeed OCD and not just some weird phase I was going through. If she had known what was to come, she feels that she would have been better prepared for when my OCD came back, and maybe she could have stopped it from getting so bad. We will never know for sure, but it seems reasonable to us that stopping OCD before it gets too big is much easier than trying to deal with it after it has grown into something monstrous. After all, isn't it easier to deal with the sparks before the flames grow, coalesce, and form a full-fledged fire?

With your experience in dealing with OCD, you will be well prepared to deal with any OCD "sparks" a child of yours may have. You will know what to do, who to ask for help, and how to outfox their OCD.

How do I tell someone what OCD is and what it's like to have it?

Informing others about the true nature of OCD is integral in the recovery process. If your parents or anyone else around you do not understand what OCD is really like, then informing them is up to you. You must convince them that OCD is a devastating and a real mental disorder. Otherwise, how are you to get treatment?

There are several ways to define OCD, such as an official one (the one mental health professionals use): *OCD is an anxiety disorder that is characterized by recurrent, unwanted thoughts, images, or impulses (obsessions) and/or repetitive behaviors (compulsions). Repetitive behaviors such as hand washing, counting, checking, or cleaning are often performed with the hope of preventing the obsessive thoughts or making them go away. Performing these so-called "rituals," however, provides only temporary relief, and not performing them markedly increases anxiety.* This description is long and you will most likely lose the attention of the person you are explaining OCD to. This description also doesn't help people really understand what OCD feels like. In my experience, people just can't understand why I can't forget or ignore the thoughts. I know (because researchers have actually studied this) that all people have experienced thoughts similar to mine (and yours). The difference is that non-

OCDers can dismiss the thoughts as unimportant, whereas those of us who have OCD can't. In fact, our minds tell us to focus on the thoughts and give those thoughts importance.

Another way to describe OCD to others is to explain that it is a brain disorder. The experts in OCD have found that the brains of us who have OCD function differently from those without OCD. They did this by using complicated brain scanners that can detect what areas of a brain are firing and what areas are quiet. Apparently, there are areas of our OCD-affected brains that are often working when they should be quiet. There was even a study using the brain scanners that found that relatives of those who have OCD had brain changes resembling OCD even though they didn't have any OCD symptoms. What all this means is that OCD results from a real problem in the brain and is as much a mental disorder as schizophrenia or depression. Furthermore, OCD (and many other mental disorders) should be treated with the same attention and respect as that of other conditions, such as epilepsy (repeated seizures in the brain) or diabetes (resulting from a lack of insulin from the pancreas).

Yet another way to explain OCD is to use analogies. Personally, this is my favorite way, and the one that works best to describe what OCD feels like. All of us feel fear and panic at one time or another because of certain things that happen to us. With OCD, however, these feeling are not only stuck within us, but they rewind themselves over and over again. Here are some of mine and Dr. M's ideas about what OCD is and what it feels like.

- OCD feels like the moment when you lose something very important to you (eg, wallet, purse, necklace, homework assignment) and you don't know where it is. How many of us can feel calm again until we can search for it?
- OCD feels like the moment when you are driving and suddenly see that another car is very close to you. It is going to hit you? Is there going to be a wreck?
- OCD feels like the moment you turn around in a place like a store and suddenly notice that your child isn't standing by you any-more (this one's Dr. M's). You know that your heart rate isn't going to decrease until you find your child.
- OCD feels like the moment when you sud-denly realize you have touched something hot (eg, stove, hot water, fire), and the pain is just starting to shoot up your fingers.
- OCD feels like the second you realize you have done something extremely embarrass-

ing (eg, farted in public, walked around with your zipper open, said something bad about someone who was standing behind you).

If you really want to tell others what OCD feels like, try having them remember a time when they experienced something uncomfortable. Have them remember what physical and mental signs they had, such as a fast heart beat, breaking out in sweat, dizziness, or difficulty breathing. Then, tell them to imagine having this experience hundreds of times a day, every day, with no end in sight. How well could they take it?

better for a while. But, it never lasts long before the thoughts come back. I think I may have obsessive compulsive disorder, and I need your help.

I don't know what your parents will say or do after you tell them about your obsessions and how you need their help. If you are lucky, they will spring into action, run to the nearest computer and lookup OCD, or grab the phone and call the nearest mental health center. If, however, they just stare blankly at you or try in any way to diminish the importance of your obsessions, then you need to keep trying. Your health and your future depend on it. Don't let them talk you into dismissing your thoughts as "just a phase you will grow out of, or you just need to stop playing those awful video games and everything will be all right, or you are just doing this to get attention." If you have to, stand on a chair and yell, throw something, or pitch the biggest fit you can. You need to do whatever it takes to get their attention.

your OCD, then I'm sure they have noticed your red, chapped hands and have repeatedly asked you to use lotion on them. They may also wonder why you need so much reassurance about small things that happen and are getting impatient with you every time you ask for that reassurance. As hard as we OCDers try to hide our symptoms, there are always several that slip through.

I wish that I could help you tell your parents about your thoughts and help you make plans for what to do next. Since I can't do it face to face, I decided to write down some ideas for you to use.

Mom and Dad, I need you to both sit down because I need to talk to you. For some time now I have had these strange thoughts that pop into my head almost constantly. I don't know why I have them, but they make me very upset. Sometimes, I also have images, like pictures. These thoughts and images are not right, and I need you to understand what I am going through. Mostly, these thoughts are about sex (or whatever your OCD centers on) but are not the normal sex thoughts that teenagers have. These are bad, and I don't know how to describe them. They make me feel guilty, dirty, and like I don't deserve to have good things happen to me. I don't know how to deal with these thoughts so I wash my hands (or take a shower, change my clothes, repeat words or numbers in my head — any one or more of endless compulsions that OCDers have). For some reason, doing these things helps me feel a little

How do I tell my parents about my ob-sessions?

First, you need to face the reason why you haven't told them yet. Maybe you are afraid they won't understand. Or perhaps, you fear that they won't know what to do or will do the wrong thing in trying to help you. Parents are used to fixing their children's problems and may not know what to do when faced with something as bizarre as OCD. Today's parents are also often very busy with their work and trying to keep the household running. They may not have the luxury of time to figure out what is happening to you. It is also possible that there is already so much stress in your home that you don't want to add to it by revealing your OCD. Whatever the reasons are for your not telling, you need get over them and tell your parents. You need help, and you need it as quickly as you can get it. And, you can't get help without your parents knowing.

There is a good chance that your parents, and anyone else who lives closely with you, have already noticed some of your OCD behaviors. You probably ask them to do things that most people wouldn't need to have done for them. Maybe your mother has mentioned to you several times about the huge amounts of laundry you generate or the amount of soap you use. If you are a hand washer as part of cause of certain things that happen to us. With OCD, however, these feeling are not only stuck within us, but they rewind themselves over and over again. Here are some of mine and Dr. M's ideas about what OCD is and what it feels like.

- OCD feels like the moment when you lose something very important to you (eg, wallet, purse, necklace, homework assignment) and you don't know where it is. How many of us can feel calm again until we can search for it?
- OCD feels like the moment when you are driving and suddenly see that another car is very close to you. It is going to hit you? Is there going to be a wreck?
- OCD feels like the moment you turn around in a place like a store and suddenly notice that your child isn't standing by you anymore (this one's Dr. M's). You know that your heart rate isn't going to decrease until you find your child.
- OCD feels like the moment when you suddenly realize you have touched something hot (eg, stove, hot water, fire), and the pain is just starting to shoot up your fingers.
- OCD feels like the second you realize you have done something extremely embarrass-

ing (eg, farted in public, walked around with your zipper open, said something bad about someone who was standing behind you).

If you really want to tell others what OCD feels like, try having them remember a time when they experienced something uncomfortable. Have them remember what physical and mental signs they had, such as a fast heart beat, breaking out in sweat, dizziness, or difficulty breathing. Then, tell them to imagine having this experience hundreds of times a day, every day, with no end in sight. How well could they take it?

What do I say when my parents tell me to "just get over it or just stop it, you know you can?"

I bet that almost one hundred percent of parents whose kids have OCD will tell their kids this in the beginning. Even Dr. M, during my first months of having OCD, told me that if I just work harder at it or if I try harder to ignore my thoughts that I could be symptom free. I mean, this makes sense, doesn't it? We all have weird thoughts that pass through our minds from time to time. In fact, when surveys are done on normal people (ie, non-OCDers) they often admit to having thoughts that are similar to OCD obsessions. In other words, every one of us has strange sexual thoughts, thoughts about harming or even killing someone, or unnerving thoughts about germs. The difference for those of us who have OCD is that our thoughts somehow get stuck in our heads. What our parents or anyone else around us don't understand is that we can't get these thoughts unstuck like they can. They have learned to ignore these thoughts and just throw them out like they are nothing more than a piece of junk mail. We OCDers, however, can't do this; it's like we're stuck on thinking that every piece of junk mail is important and can't be thrown away without something bad happening. We just can't throw it away like everyone else can. We would love to, but we can't.

Another thing that parents (and the general population for that matter) need to realize is that OCD is a mental disorder just as much as posttraumatic stress disorder, depression, bipolar disorder, or schizophrenia. Furthermore, it's like any physical disorder like diabetes, epilepsy, or cancer. No one in their right mind would ever tell a diabetic to "just get over it." Or, tell a cancer patient that "if they just work harder, that they would get better." We now know that OCD is a brain disorder and that there are specific areas of the brain that fail to work like they should. To get this faulty wiring corrected and working normally takes a lot of hard work. No amount of yelling, cajoling, bribing, punishing, or applying discipline will fix OCD. If it did, then we would all be cured of OCD very quickly.

Some of us who have the faulty wiring of OCD, however, are lucky and never have any severe OCD symptoms. Why this happens to some of us and not others has yet to be determined. Perhaps, for some of us, our environments provided the necessary protection, whereas for others, it tipped us over into OCD. Dr. M has always wondered if her generally intense approach to life may have contributed to my OCD. During my early years, she was in residency and then practiced pediatrics in a small hospital. She was always busy and often didn't have time to spend with me. I have always been proud of how hard she worked and of how many people she helped. When we look back, however, we can see how this situation could have contributed to the sparking of my OCD. She was busy with her patients at a time when I needed her. At the same time, however, I know that having intensity helps us succeed in life. Dr. M's intensity helped her get through medical school, residency, and her pediatric practice. We will never know for sure if this situation, or any other that occurred in our home, caused my OCD. It's probably not worth too much of our time trying to figure it out.

Why your parents are having a difficult time respecting OCD for what it is may also come from how they have been exposed to it. I have often been dismayed at how loosely the words obsessive and compulsive are used. I have actually read blogs asking questions such as "What is your OCD?" People write back and list things like calories, pet peeves (eg, "I can't stand it when so and so does this"), volume on televisions, grammar, and many other things that are definitely not true OCD. I have even had people tell me that they have OCD or OCD tendencies. But, when I ask further, I often find that they don't really have OCD but instead, are passionate about or have worries about something. I have even read comics and T-shirts that poke fun at OCD, like it is something that we all should laugh at. Imagine what would happen if cartoonists target some other condition like obesity, muscular dystrophy, or epilepsy. For some reason, calling attention to most other conditions is considered politically incorrect. Why is OCD any different?

It is crucial that you convince your parents of OCD's reality. I wish I could help you explain to your parents that OCD is real, complex, and difficult to treat. Since I can't be physically there, I will try to give you some ideas here.

Mom and Dad, you constantly tell me that I can get over OCD if I just put my mind to it. It's like you think that OCD is not real but is something I just made up to cause trouble. This is impossible because OCD results from a brain disorder, which means that parts of my brain fail to work like they should. What this means is that my obsessions are not under my control. I wish I could stop them because they cause me and you so much pain. I need help from you and from a professional who has a lot of experience in treating OCD. I need you to understand that OCD is as much a disorder as posttraumatic stress disorder or depression. I need to be under the guidance of someone who understands what I am going through and knows how to help me defeat OCD.

I hope these ideas help. But, don't be surprised if you have to keep trying to convince your parents about OCD and what it does.

After I've been diagnosed with OCD, what can my parents do at home to help me?

There are many things that your parents can do to help you, but it is also equally likely that there are many things they need to stop doing. In many cases, mine included, parents or other family members unintentionally make OCD worse, even though they think they are helping. Before she understood the finer points of OCD, Dr. M would often reassure me whenever I would say "bad thought." I said this whenever, which was over 100 times a day at my worst times, I had a sexual thought, image, or feeling. I know that it was hard for Dr. M not to reassure me when she saw how much pain I was in, but it was important that she not do it. It was like every time I got my requested reassurance, my OCD fed off of it and became stronger. There were also other times when Dr. M enabled (the professional term for doing what OCD requests) my OCD. I would badger her into opening a door for me or insist that she wash yet another set of sheets or make her refill the soap dispenser for the second time in a day because I had used up all the soap again. She learned quickly, however, not to listen to these OCD requests. Your parents will need to learn the same, and the quicker they do it, the better for you.

Even though it's important your parents stop enabling your OCD, it may not be the best thing to have them do so abruptly. It is possible that if they immediately stop listening to your OCD commands, you might stop functioning. In my situation, I know that Dr. M sometimes gave in and did what my OCD asked so that I could get to my homework or study for an upcoming test. There were many instances that if she had stood her ground and refused to do what was asked of her, I probably wouldn't have gotten my work done. I would have become so angry and upset because of my OCD that I couldn't have focused on my schoolwork. Dr. M knew that good grades were important to my future. Even though she also knew that beating back my OCD was critical, she would somehow try to balance these two competing goals. You and your parents may need to agree on what OCD behaviors they should enable for a while so that you can keep moving forward in your life. Just remember, however, that the more you force them into enabling your OCD, the longer and harder it will be for you to completely destroy your OCD.

What else can your parents do to help you? There are many things. They can, for example, try to lessen the stress in the home environment. Stress is one factor that is known to worsen OCD symptoms. If yelling is a normal way of communicating between your family members, for example, then finding a new and more respectful way of talking with each other would definitely help. Parents often argue about many issues, and I know that OCD can be a frequent topic that causes arguments. Nobody knows for sure what to do when OCD shows up, but everyone seems to have an opinion. One of your parents may insist that all you need is more discipline, whereas the other thinks you need to see a psychiatrist. One wants to increase the number of chores you do at home, and the other thinks you need a break from chores so that you can focus on your homework. OCD can cause many areas of contention between your parents. But, if the goal is to have you beat your OCD so that you can have a great life, then they need to stop arguing with each other and join forces to help you win back your life.

Another thing your parents should give you to help you fight OCD is simply their time. OCD is a complicated disorder, and it does different things to each one of us who has it. To figure out all that OCD is doing to you and how to unravel what it has done takes a lot of time and patience. I know for a fact that I couldn't have gotten my life back if Dr. M hadn't given up a lot of her time. I was lucky that she was able to do this. She decided early on in my OCD that she would pull back from her career as a pediatrician so that she could focus on helping me. I know that not all parents can afford to do what Dr. M did, but I'm sure that if they work at it, they can find time for you. Ask them; beg them if you have to.

Once my OCD is gone, will I then have a normal life?

To defeat OCD, both you and your parents need to understand that it will take a long time. Everyone needs to prepare for the long haul. Sometimes, I think that understanding and then defeating OCD is like training and then running an ultra-marathon through some desolate desert. You often wonder if you have the stamina and the heart to really deal with it all.

Also, your work towards recovery might not be done even after you have beaten back your OCD. OCD causes a lot of havoc in our lives. It's like a tornado that rips apart your house. After it's gone, you are relieved and thankful to still be alive, but then, you realize that you now have a broken house that will take a long time and effort to repair. OCD rips apart your life in many ways; perhaps because of OCD, you have poor grades or have even had to stop your education for a while. You may have lost friendships along the way or have worn out your parents to the extent that they now just want to go on with their lives and not deal with your problems any longer. During the time OCD had me down, I did all right with regards to school, but not so well with social relationships. I had a hard time keeping my old friends and making new ones. Sometimes, I couldn't even talk to some of my family members like I wanted to. Also, I realize now that many people had judged me based on my OCD behaviors and not on who I really am. As teenagers we need these social interactions to grow up normal, and OCD keeps us from getting them. So what are we to do? Defeat OCD, pick up the pieces of our lives, and move forward. If we don't, OCD still wins.

Once my OCD was under control, Dr. M and I started to repair the damage that had been caused by OCD. Her first steps were to let family members know what had been going on with me. We hadn't told anyone about my OCD. I hadn't wanted anyone else to know because I was too embarrassed and didn't want anyone to think less of me. Dr. M had told me this was ridiculous, but I still didn't want others to know. We didn't tell everything right away, especially the part about me having sexual obsessions. We did this, not because we are ashamed of those obsessions, but because sexual obsessions are too difficult to explain and because sex is a topic that often causes embarrassment. In time, we explained more about my OCD and what we had been through to defeat it. Now that they all know about my OCD, I feel that they better understand me and that our relationships have grown stronger.

Repairing friendships, especially when you're a teenager, is much harder than repairing family relationships. Your family is stuck with you, but friends often come and go. I have also found that we teenagers rarely have the patience for anyone who is out of the ordinary or just plain weird. Those people are just too uncool, and we certainly don't want to associate with them. I know that I behaved differently from most teenagers, even though I tried desperately to hide my OCD. What were my friends to think when they saw my red, chapped hands that had resulted from constantly washing, when I always failed to remember my homework, when I failed to join in their sex jokes or in their conversations about girls, or when they saw the pain in my face? I was not fun or cool to be around and eventually, many of my friends drifted away. But, now that I've defeated my OCD, I have reconnected with some friends. These friendships are not as close as they could be, but at least, I have started rebuilding what OCD has taken away from me. Dr. M also says that college will give me an opportunity to start over. Being in a new environment that is filled with people who haven't seen my OCD-driven behaviors will allow me the chance to finally develop the friendships I want.

OCD sucks up way too much of our lives. It drains away our energy, motivation, and time. We try to move forward but find ourselves mired in OCD mud. Sometimes, I felt my life was like a car engine that was stuck in neutral but had the gas pedal to the floor. All I could manage to do was to sit in one place and rev the engine. And, at the same time that I was stuck in neutral, I could only watch as my friends, cousins, and classmates whizzed by me, going on with their lives. Now that I'm finally out of the mud and in gear, I find that I am somewhat behind where I should be. Had OCD left me alone I could have been more experienced in social relationships, more organized about my future, and more confident about who I am. This used to worry me, but then I realized: What good would that do? Nothing. Whenever I start to fret over how I think someone I know has done better than me, I think about a quote that Dr. M found. "I'll meet you at the finish line." I may not get there first, but I will get there. And, so will you.

Aren't you embarrassed to tell others that you have OCD and that it involves sexual obsessions?

At this point, I am not embarrassed to tell others about my sexual obsessions. Was there a time when I was embarrassed? Sure, it was when I first had these obsessions and before I understood what was happening to me. Even now, when I talk to others about OCD, I don't mention the specifics. In fact, most of the time, they don't ask. I think they just assume that I'm a germ phobe who needs to incessantly wash his hands. In other words, they assume that I am like the OCDers who are most commonly portrayed in the media. This is not because I feel shameful about having sexual obsessions; it's just that I don't want to deal with anyone's ignorance. If I talked openly, it's certainly possible that someone would mistake me for being a pedophile (because of my sexual obsessions regarding children) or a sex pervert rather than someone who has OCD. I have learned that there are many people who take facts out of context and falsely transform them into something larger. In my opinion, these people are the ones who rarely understand those around them and are honestly, not worth my limited amount of time. In fact, I feel sorry for these people because they are missing out on knowing some incredible people.

Chances are that someone will read this book and think it's funny that I have problems with sexual issues. It is even possible that some of my classmates, especially the ones who don't know me well, will talk behind my back and make jokes at my expense. What would I tell them?

- Who are you to judge me? You know nothing about me and what it's like to have OCD. There are many of us who have mental disorders. The man throwing a fit on the street may be suffering from bipolar disorder or is a solider, who has severe posttraumatic stress disorder because he has just returned from combat. You can't simply assume that this person is a jerk because you fail to understand the full story of their actions. The same goes for me. As Confucius says, treat others just as you would want others to treat you. You never know, someday you might need me to help you out.

- If that doesn't work, I might just pick them up and slam them into a locker. That should get their attention (just kidding, Dr. M).

My advice is not to tell others the specifics of your obsessions. They won't get it, and they might even cause you some additional headaches. I don't say this because I have any shame or embarrassment about these types of obsessions. The problem lies with others and their ignorance.

Should I tell my friends about my OCD?

Dr. M and I decided early on that we would not let many others know about my OCD. She especially worried about the sexual nature of my obsessions and thought that it was better for me if we kept quiet. I think that this was a wise decision. Not many adults, let alone teenagers, have the patience to really learn what OCD is and what it does to those who are afflicted with it.

Dr. M and I also worried about the possibility of someone using my OCD to hurt me. We teenagers can sometimes be brutal with each other. We often tease, mock, put down, and generally shun anyone who is different. I don't know why we do this; maybe it has something to do with how our brains are developing. Dr. M has often said that she couldn't wait until my frontal lobes came on line. The frontal lobes are that part of our brains (generally located behind our eyes) that we use to help us plan, make good judgments, and think abstractly. Because of our age, we teenagers don't often use, or even have good access to, this part of our brains. In fact, it has been shown that the frontal lobes are not fully functioning until we reach our early 20's. And, there have even been court cases involving teenagers in which this immaturity of the frontal lobe has been successfully used as a defense. What does all this have to do with OCD? Simple, your peers may not understand your OCD and how much pain it's causing you. Instead, they may just see the weird parts of it and find it funny. In other words, your friends just might make you worse.

If you do decide to let your friends know about your OCD, keep in mind that you don't have to tell them everything. Most people today have at least heard of OCD, thanks mainly to some recent TV programs. Chances are your friends will just think you are some fanatic hand washer (because this is the most common type of compulsion and the one often seen in programs). They might even tell you that they "have a touch of OCD." I didn't tell any of my friends about my OCD until I was over the worst of it. I'm not sure why I even mentioned it when I did, but I think it was because I had fought it so long and that it was somehow a part of me. It also didn't seem honest to at least recognize OCD and its role in my life. And, I think I was also tired of hiding it.

Have I told any of my friends that my OCD is mainly sexual? No, I didn't, and I don't plan to. Sex is a topic that is so difficult to talk about and to understand. Even though sexual feelings and impulses are in all of us and even directs a good part of our lives, we remain uncomfortable talking openly about it. Mention sex to someone, and chances are that they will blush, start stammering, or start cracking jokes about it. I don't know why we treat sex this way, but I think it stems from how powerful sexual feelings are in us. Sex in humans, like in any other species, evolved as a necessity to keep us going. If we want to survive as a species, we need to have sex and because of this, we evolved many ways to keep sexual feelings up front in our lives. From an evolutionary standpoint, it has been only recently that we evolved the consciousness to try to understand sex on a more civilized level. What I'm trying to say here is that sex is too complicated to talk about in a normal away, let alone combine it with something as difficult as OCD.

I know that some of my friends suspected that something was up with me when my OCD was at its worst. They knew I was withdrawing from them and that I often seemed upset. If they asked me what was going on, I was quick to dismiss them and to hide what was going on with me. I have thought about telling some of my friends about my OCD and how it had affected me. Here is some of what I would say.

- *A: Sorry I didn't invite you over more often. I wanted to, but I knew that my OCD would get in the way and that we wouldn't have any fun. My head was so messed up for a while that I thought that you would somehow contaminate my room and if that happened,* then I wouldn't have anywhere safe to sleep.

- *B: Sorry that I had to ask you over and over again about homework. My OCD thoughts often kept me from hearing what you or anyone else was saying to me. I know that you often got annoyed at me because of this. I wasn't trying to be weird or lazy. I just couldn't help it.*

- *C: Sorry I walked away every time you cracked a joke about sex or girls. I wasn't being rude to you. Your jokes triggered my OCD, and I couldn't handle it.*

- *D: Sorry I stopped talking to you and started walking away whenever I saw you. You are a girl and at one time, anything to do with a female would trigger my OCD symptoms.*

- *E: Sorry I refused to come to your house whenever you asked me. You were always one who talked a lot about sex, and I knew that if I ever came over that I couldn't handle it very well.*

- *F: Sorry I often acted angry with you or interrupted you when you were talking. Sometimes, what you were talking about (usually something about sex) bothered me to the point that I couldn't handle it.*

- *A,B,C,D,E, and F: Sorry I couldn't be a good friend to you. I know that you all have gone on and have found other friends. But, I wanted you all to know that it was because of my OCD that I couldn't be around you anymore. You did nothing wrong, and*

I hope that now you understand me a little better.

And, finally to the parents of my friends.

- *Mr. A: Sorry that I may have acted different around you. My anxiety often shows through even though I try very hard to hide it. I know that my behavior seemed weird to you at times. My OCD often causes me to act nervous around those I don't know well, and I have difficulty making eye contact. I can assure you that I am not a troublemaker and will not in any way be a bad influence on your son. And, I am definitely not on drugs.*

- *Mrs. B: Sorry that I often called your house because I needed to talk to your son about my homework. My OCD often caused me to lose my homework or resulted in my not paying attention in class. I know you found me annoying at times, but I didn't know how to tell anyone that I needed some extra help.*

Should I tell my teachers about my OCD?

I didn't tell my teachers mainly because of the sexual nature of my obsessions. Dr. M said she always worried that if my teachers knew of my sexual obsessions that one of them might actually call the authorities who deal with child abuse, thinking that I had been sexually abused. In other words, she feared their ignorance. I also wanted, like most other teenagers, to be viewed as normal (whatever that happens to be). I didn't want to be thought of as weak. I also wanted to know that what I had accomplished was because of me and not because some teachers felt sorry for me. Maybe this wouldn't have happened, but at the time, I wasn't willing to take the chance.

School is very difficult to deal with if you have OCD. For me, OCD stood in front of a lot of possible school progress that I could have made. I actually used homework papers or pages from textbooks as barriers to use to open doors with and touch things that I didn't want to touch. For example, I didn't study for my ACT standardized test because I had used a portion of the study book as paper to touch things, such as door handles, that I was convinced had been contaminated with semen. Because of this, I was losing a lot of homework and obviously, found this failure unfair because it was due to the stress of

OCD. I also struggled frequently with teachers in regards to being late to class or having to often leave class. In fact, I had been late so many times during my sophomore year of high school (one of the low points of my OCD) that I had received several detentions and eventually, had to spend four hours at school on a Saturday as punishment. At this time, I was taking so much time in between classes washing my hands that I was late to almost all of my classes. I also was having many conflicts with a few teachers who questioned me frequently about leaving class to go to the bathroom. Also, because of my OCD, I often appeared as if I wasn't paying any attention to what the teachers were saying. It is hard to pay attention when your thoughts are stuck on obsessions. Because of these conflicts, I developed poor relationships with some teachers. They didn't enjoy having me as a student, and I didn't enjoy having them as teachers. Most of them are nice people and good teachers. They just didn't think of the possibility that I had something else (like OCD) going on.

To avoid having to waste most of my Saturdays in detention, Dr. M and I decided that we should tell the vice principal of my school about my OCD. We explained to him why I was always late to class and how punishing me wasn't going to stop my behaviors. He was very understanding, and my tardies were erased. In this case, telling someone at school about OCD helped relieve me of stress and made my life significantly easier.

I think that you should tell your teachers about your OCD if telling them relieves stress in your life. I didn't tell them about my sexual obsessions because of the societal view on sex in general. Just mentioning that I had a disorder along with something about sex would immediately have sent up red flags and scared people. Also, telling them in depth about my particular OCD wouldn't have had any more effect that couldn't be gained by just telling them generally about OCD.

I have often thought about telling some of my past teachers about things I may have done to annoy them, and why I did the things I did. I wasn't purposely trying to annoy them, but I know that's what they often thought. Here is some of what I would say.

- *Mr. A: Sorry I was always late to your class. I really tried to get there on time, but because of my OCD, I needed to wash my hands.*
- *Mr. B: Sorry I left your class so many times. I just had to wash my hands, or I wouldn't have been able to continue working in your class.*
- *Ms C: Sorry I looked like I wasn't paying attention. I was dealing with constant obsessions, which made it hard for me to focus on what you were saying.*
- *Mrs. D: Sorry I had to ask you constantly for extra*

homework papers. My OCD often told me the first ones were contaminated, and I had to throw them away.

- *Coach E: Sorry I caused you problems. I couldn't always show up for practice because of my OCD. I really did want to participate, and I didn't mean to be disrespectful to you.*
- *Mr. F: Sorry I had so much trouble memorizing my music for band. I always felt that it was contaminated and either washed it (of course, you know what happens when paper is washed) or threw it away.*
- *Mr./Mrs./MS A,B,C,D,E, and F: Sorry that I caused you problems by not being prepared. There were times when I lost track of my homework and even my textbooks because of OCD.*

And, finally to Mr. G: Thanks. Somehow my quirkiness never bothered you, and you helped me a lot. You probably don't remember this, but you stopped me in the hallway one time and complimented me on something I had done for your class. I can never thank you enough for that; you helped pull me through.

WHAT DO I SAY TO PEOPLE WHO TELL ME THAT I DON'T SEEM LIKE I HAVE OCD?

The first time I told one of my friends that I have OCD he said, "Ha, you don't look like you have OCD." My response was simply to ask him what he thought someone who has OCD looked like. Of course, he didn't have a good answer. The people around us rarely see our OCD because we OCDers are extraordinarily good at hiding our symptoms. We know that our obsessions are not grounded in reality and that our compulsions do nothing but temporarily relieve our anxieties. We know that our thinking and our actions are weird. And, we go to extreme lengths to hide that weirdness from our friends, teachers, employers, and even certain family members. Only with those we have complete confidence in do we let down our guard and let our OCD show. In fact, our symptoms often dramatically increase when we are alone or with those we trust. It's like OCD builds up a pressure in us that we fight to keep contained and when we are finally where we can let it go, it explodes.

In my case, my explosions were mainly around Dr. M and no one else. I know this often caused frustration for her because no one else ever really saw my OCD. Whenever she would mention my struggles with OCD and her difficulties in helping me deal with it, she was often met with skepticism and even dismissal. She often heard things like, "Ray behaves fine with me; I don't see what you are talking about, he looks good whenever I'm around him; or You must be doing something wrong because Ray acts normally whenever I'm around him." It was like no one believed her and that the problems were with her and not with my OCD.

Now that my OCD is in a much better place, I am more open about what Dr. M and I have been through. We know from our experience that most people don't "get" OCD right away and require a lot of explaining before they can understand it. We hope that by talking to others about OCD and by writing about it that we can help bridge the gap between what the public thinks OCD is and what it really is. So, what do you do when your friends say that you don't look like someone who has OCD? If you can, tell them. Tell them all about OCD and what you have been through. Make them listen, for your sake and for the sake of all of us who have OCD.

Did you ever consider committing suicide during the worst times of your OCD?

I never had the true intent to commit suicide during the times when my OCD was out of control. Dr. M, however, worried about it a lot and always kept a close watch on me. I never had a definite plan by which to commit suicide, let alone tried it. There were times, though, when I would think about how hard life was with OCD and how easier it would be to stop living. Even though I knew that OCD was making my life poor and dreary, I also knew that giving up would represent the ultimate victory for OCD. One of my strong points is that I don't like thinking of myself as a loser. In a way, this thinking protected me and helped me in my fight against OCD. But, I can certainly understand why someone would want to commit suicide instead of living a life dominated by OCD. OCD sucks the fun out of life; it makes you question practically every action you make. Every step you take is filled with fear or guilt, and almost every moment in your life you have this mysterious force that sways your every decision. It is simply not a good way to live.

Another way I dealt with any suicidal thoughts was by thinking about the pain that my loved ones would feel if I did kill myself. Having OCD taught me more than I ever wanted to know about mental pain. How could I inflict a similar pain on others? I also knew that suicide would be a cowardly and self-ish way to deal with my problems. With the help of my loved ones, I knew that I could defeat OCD and go on to have a good life.

What should you do if you don't have loved ones who can provide you with the needed support? Your journey may be harder, but you can still do it. Look for support anywhere you can find it (eg, teachers, friends, neighbors, support groups, mental health professionals). Try again and again to explain what you need to your loved ones. If nothing else works, get a dog, a cat, or even a fish. You need someone. Once you develop a good relationship with some-one (even if it's a pet), it's like you become mentally indebted to that person. You owe it to them not to cause them pain. And, I can't think of anything more painful than experiencing a friend's or a loved one's suicide.

How will my OCD be diagnosed when I see a psychiatrist (or other mental health professional)?

Like most mental disorders, there are no blood or brain tests that can accurately diagnose OCD. Sometimes, I wish there was a test that we OCDers could take. That way, we could show those doubters around us that we do indeed have a real problem with our brains. We could point to the test every time someone says to us things like: "You just need some more discipline; you could stop this silliness anytime you wanted; and you're just doing this to get attention." We could wave our test result at them and say "See, our problems are just as real and out of our control as someone who has asthma, diabetes, or even cancer."

Currently, OCD is diagnosed by asking someone a series of questions that pertain to OCD. Doctors who work with OCD often look for the symptoms described in a book called *The Diagnostic and Statistical Manual of Mental Disorders*. This book, which has been revised several times, is often used by clinicians to help them make diagnoses of mental disorders. The diagnostic criteria for OCD can be found in this book, and I would advise you to look it over (easy to find on the Internet) to help you decide whether or not you do have OCD. That is, if you are not sure already.

In my experience, seeing a psychiatrist (a medical doctor who specializes in mental disorders) for the first time is not fun. At my first visit, I talked with the psychiatrist alone, which was a strange experience for me. Before this, one of my parents had always been with me when I saw a doctor. I also found it very uncomfortable to answer all the personal questions that I was asked. And, I had to explain the specifics about my OCD, which meant that I had to talk about my sexual obsessions. In other words, I had to talk openly about a very difficult, personal, and frightening topic to someone who I had just met. It was not easy. To help me through this first discussion, I reminded myself that this psychiatrist was trained specifically to help those who have mental disorders and that nothing I had to say would surprise him. He had probably heard it all before with regards to OCD.

There is a good chance that your psychiatrist (or other mental health professional) will request to see your parent(s) without you. This gives your parents a chance to speak openly and to tell what they have noticed about you without feeling that they are embarrassing or insulting you in any way. Also, I know that I couldn't have dealt with sitting there and listening to Dr. M describe my OCD symptoms. It would have been too tempting for me to argue with her when she talked about my illogical thoughts and actions. "I am not that crazy," I would have probably shouted, and we would have ended up spending our session arguing with each other.

To wrap up the session, everyone (you, your parents, and the psychiatrist) will probably meet together to discuss your diagnosis and what to do about it. Any number of ideas may be presented at this point. For some, a recommendation for medication may be made and others may be given a referral to a psychologist for therapy. In severe cases, like in those when someone is thought to be suicidal, then immediate hospitalization in a psychiatry unit will be advised. I left my visit with a prescription for an antidepressant and a recommendation to see a psychologist.

Is it possible to have other conditions in addition to OCD?

Unfortunately, it is highly likely that you will eventually be diagnosed with another condition in addition to your OCD. Studies on OCD have estimated that between ½ to ¾ of us will have an additional diagnosis, such as depression, attention deficit disorder, general anxiety disorder, or panic disorder. The most common of these extra diagnoses is depression. In fact, some studies suggest that almost 80% of those who have OCD will also have depression at some point in their lives. I definitely have felt depressed to the point that all I wanted to do was to sleep the days away. During this time, I had no energy, no desire to go forward with life, and no hope for my future. It's not surprising to me that I felt this depression. Having OCD wears you down; even fighting OCD through therapy can take a lot out of you. And, when depression strikes, it becomes even harder to effectively deal with your OCD. It's like you now have two enemies to fight instead of just one.

There are also smaller and less-easily diagnosed problems that often come up with us OCDers. Maybe this is true for everyone, but having OCD somehow makes these extra problems even more difficult. I, for example, have problems with impulsivity. I act quickly without thinking and as a result, have broken or lost things. I ride bikes fast and have broken several. Recently, I even broke the rear view mirror on my friend's car (long story I how managed to do that) and the computer screen on a new school laptop. I'm not sure, but think I had left it too close to my desk ledge, and it fell off. These accidents, of course, cause problems for me in terms of my friendships, my family relationships, and in expenses (just ask Dr. M who bails me out every time). Dr. M. thinks my impulsivity, even though not directly related to my OCD, comes from problems in brain areas that are close to those affected by OCD. In other words, whatever process that caused my OCD may have also caused problems with impulsivity.

If you have other diagnoses in addition to your OCD, it means that you will need to work even harder. You might need additional medications or need to focus your therapies on more than just OCD. As for my impulsivity, Dr. M and I are now targeting it and am in the process of working out the details. We couldn't work too hard on dealing with my impulsiveness when my OCD symptoms were in full force. But, now that my OCD is quiet, we have the time and energy to figure out all my other problems.

Did you name your OCD like it suggests in some OCD books?

We named my OCD "Raytard." Calling my OCD this was something Dr. M and I came up with when I first experienced my major OCD symptoms (around age 11). Apparently, naming your OCD is an idea that is common in many books on OCD, and we found it helped us. I hesitated to include the name Raytard in this book due to the offensive nature of the name to people who actually have mental retardation. However, I also wanted to tell my story as it actually happened. The actual name came from combining the word retard and my name, Ray. At the time, we actually thought we were being quite clever.

Dr. M and I named my OCD to make it something we hated. Although it was pretty obvious that having OCD was not a good thing, it was necessary to constantly remind me that OCD was bad and was trying to trick me. Without some kind of evil name to call my OCD, I might have given in to the thoughts more, because I would have had more trouble distinguishing between real thoughts and OCD-related thoughts. Of course, I could have just referred to my OCD as, well, my OCD. But, somehow giving it a more personalized name made it into something easier to fight against. It also gave Dr. M a way to talk to me about OCD. She would often says things like "Is Raytard telling you to wash your hands? or You know, that thought is nothing more than another of Raytard's tricks." Sometimes, Dr. M would even ask me why I listened to Raytard so much instead of her. She would remind me that Raytard was trying to destroy me, whereas she was trying to help me. There were even many times when we symbolically killed Raytard. We have set him on fire, repeatedly stomped on him, threw him off many, different bridges, and stabbed him with any handy sharp object. We did these things, because the more we demonized Raytard, the easier it became to hate my OCD. And, with that hatred, came a desire to get better.

Dr. M. also thinks that naming my OCD helped her to deal with it. Many times my OCD tried her patience to the point she resorted to yelling at me. "Stop washing," she would yell or "Why can't you just understand that there is nothing to worry about?" Of course, this didn't help. After all, if yelling cured OCD, then all us would have been cured a long time ago. With my OCD renamed as Raytard, she could then say after losing her cool with me, "You know I'm not yelling at you. I'm yelling at Raytard." Somehow, it helped diffuse whatever situation we were facing and allowed Dr. M to calm back down. In a way, she could get her frustrations out by yelling, but at the same time, not aggravate me.

Are there any pills that I can take to help me with my OCD?

I took medication for about 2 ½ years. My experience with medication has been varied and complicated, but the overall benefits were worth the downfalls. I first started taking Prozac (generic name: fluoxetine) about half way through my freshmen year in high school after my OCD symptoms had gotten out of control and were affecting people around me both at home and at school. Prozac is one of the selective serotonin reuptake inhibitors (SSRIs). Its main function is to keep serotonin (an important neurotransmitter) functioning in your brain pathways longer. In other words, the serotonin in your brain works harder, which hopefully, helps you deal better with your OCD symptoms.

Anyone with a medical degree can prescribe medication for OCD. I got my medication after my first visit with a psychiatrist. But, other doctors, such as pediatricians, internists, and family practitioners, can also write prescriptions to treat OCD. Psychiatrists, however, have the most experience working with these medications. These doctors are experts in dealing with mental disorders and can more accurately determine which medication might work the best for you.

I know that many parents are hesitant about putting their kids on any type of medication, let alone one that affects mainly the brain. Even Dr. M, who had prescribed SSRIs to her patients, really didn't want me on medicine. Even though medications are generally safe to take, there are always side effects to consider. Add to this mix the fact that many teenagers don't want to take any pills, and you have some interesting dilemmas. The decision to have me take medication came mainly from Dr. M. She had watched me deteriorate over several months, and nothing she was trying was helping me. At one point, she remembers that I had a new symptom almost every day. There was something else I couldn't touch, somewhere else I couldn't walk, or something else I needed to wash. I was using a huge amount of soap both at home and school and was insisting that Dr. M wash a ridiculous amount of clothes and blankets. She realized that if something was not done, my symptoms would only continue to skyrocket and my social relationships at school and home would diminish even further. So, a decision was made to take a chance with medication.

There was no good reason why my psychiatrist chose Prozac over the other SSRIs (eg, Zoloft or Luvox). He told us that they all work pretty much the same and that Prozac was a good place to start. He also told us that if Prozac didn't work, then we would try one of the other SSRIs. And, if that one didn't work, then we would try a third one and so on. We would do this because even though these medications are all in the same category, they act differently in each person. Prozac might work well for me but not for someone else. The downside of these medications is that they can take up to several months to start working, a long time to wait when you are suffering as much as I was. Image our surprise when I started to get better within days of starting Prozac.

We're not sure why Prozac worked so quickly for me. Dr. M's theory: It wasn't so much the effect of serotonin on the brain that helped me but one of Prozac's side effects. Prozac, and SSRIs in general, are known for decreasing their taker's libido. In other words, my sex drive and presumably, my sex-related obsessions, were decreased by taking Prozac.

Prozac may have slowed down my OCD symptoms, but I didn't improve as much as Dr. M thought I could. We worked up on the Prozac dose and when that didn't help, switched to Zoloft to see if that SSRI could help me more. It really didn't; it affected me about the same as Prozac. Again, we worked up on the dose. At one time, I was taking 200 mg of Zoloft each day. Currently, I am not on any medication and am virtually OCD free.

I know that medication helped me some, but I would caution you not to rely solely on it. I believe it stopped my downward spiral and gave me time to learn how to really deal with OCD. Think of medications like a crutch; it will help you to keep going, but to heal, you need other treatments. Also, like a crutch, you should eventually no longer need it. I worked hard on my other therapies and no longer need any medication. However, I don't know what the future holds. I may need my crutch again and am willing to use it if necessary. There may even come a time when I need to permanently take medications for my OCD.

The most trouble I had with my medication was when I tried to stop it. We had planned to decrease my Zoloft slowly and for a time, I stuck with that plan. I had successfully reached a dose of 100 mg (starting at 200 mg). Then, I got impatient. I was tired of the Zoloft and was worried that it was affecting my performance in my favorite hobby of weightlifting. After reaching 100 mg, I decided to go cold turkey and completely stop taking Zoloft. BAD IDEA! I was sick for about a month, with headaches, nausea and general weakness. I even missed several days of school and overall felt terrible. I had even tried taking lesser amounts of Zoloft (eg, 75 mg) for a while, but even that didn't help. Finally, I was back to 100 mg. The next attempt to get off Zoloft was during a summer vacation, and I took it real slow. Step by step, I decreased the dose and eventually, came completely off. I still had headaches and nausea with each dose decrease, but they were less intense, and I was better able to ride them out. Withdrawal symptoms are bad enough but to deal with them while taking a full course load at school is next to impossible. My advice is that if you decide to wean your medication, pick a good time when you don't have to worry about other things.

So, should you take medication for your OCD? If your OCD is seriously affecting your life, then I think the answer is yes. Medication just might make your fight against OCD easier.

WILL I EVER NEED TO BE HOSPITALIZED BECAUSE OF MY OCD?

Maybe. I've never been. When I was at my worst, however, Dr. M seriously considered it. She says that she would have had me admitted if there had been a good psychiatric hospital nearby. But, where we live, it is hard to find well-trained mental health professionals, let alone a hospital that specializes in treating mental disorders. In many urban areas, however, the situation is different. Some cities have outpatient clinics and specialized hospitals that are designed specifically to help those who have OCD. Dr. M had actually looked into some of these clinics and had found one that was located about 100 miles from us. If I hadn't gotten better, then I'm sure that travelling to that clinic would have been our next step.

Hospitalization for those of us who have OCD is probably a good idea under certain circumstances, such as when suicide is a good possibility, when we have long refused to eat because we think our food is contaminated, when we are no longer functional because we can't leave our beds, or when our medications are so messed up that no one knows for sure what to do. In these cases (and others), a hospitalization serves to stabilize the situation and prevent someone from getting even worse. Unfortunately, this doesn't mean that someone will be cured of their

OCD when they are hospitalized. They still have a long way to go and a lot of hard work ahead of them after discharge.

For some who have OCD, there might be a need for several hospitalizations throughout their lifetime. I can see how this could happen for those who don't have good support at home, who don't have enough money for outpatient therapy or medications, and who have other diagnoses (eg, bipolar disorder or major depression) in addition to their OCD. I do think, however, that if you work hard now, educate those around you about what you need to stay healthy, and keep vigilant to OCD's tricks, then you can most likely avoid the need for hospitals.

What is the first thing I need to do to help myself get over OCD?

As strange as this may sound, the first thing you need to do is strengthen your will to fight OCD. In the beginning of my OCD, I was too afraid to do anything about it and was actually content with living with it. If I was allowed to wash my hands when I wanted to or to have someone listen to my confessions, then I was fine. Only after Dr. M repeatedly showed me how OCD was gradually taking my life, did I even try to fight it.

I would advise you to list all the ways that OCD has affected your life and then think long and hard about that list. Think about how your grades and relationships (both social and family) could have been better. Think about how much more fun you could have without OCD constantly telling you to be afraid. Think of all your future opportunities that OCD has tried to take away. And, think real hard about how it would feel to have an OCD-free life. Once you see what OCD has done to you and what it has taken from you, I hope that you get angry, really angry.

Once you see OCD for the trickster it is, then you have made a good start. You may need to constantly remind yourself that your obsessions are not grounded in reality but are formed by OCD. It might help you to think about the thousands of us who have recovered from OCD and who did it by first acknowledging that our thoughts are irrational and that our fears reside mainly in us.

To muster the strength to fight my OCD, I had to learn to think of it as my enemy. Once I did this, I quickly found the determination to fight back. Why was I just watching OCD wreck havoc on my life? Was I really that stupid and that much of a loser to let OCD have its way without a fight? I know that some of this sounds harsh, and I certainly don't mean to say that those who are struggling with OCD are losers. But, for some reason, thinking of myself as stupid or incompetent helped me rally against my OCD.

How will a psychologist help me with my OCD?

It is possible that the first person you see for your OCD is a psychologist (someone with a Ph.D. who specializes in providing therapy). Psychologists, however, are not trained to prescribe medications (like psychiatrists), but instead, are trained to help people with their mental disorders by talking with them and helping them to change how they think. A psychologist can diagnose OCD and in some cases, begin therapy without the use of any medication. If your symptoms are fairly mild and are not seriously affecting your life, then seeing a psychologist is a good place to start. For me, however, my symptoms were so severe that I couldn't have participated in therapy. Therapy can't help you unless you can concentrate on what your psychologist is telling you.

At some point with our OCD, most of us are referred to a psychologist as part of our treatment plan. A word of caution: Be certain that your psychologist is qualified and has a thorough knowledge of both the treatment and the functioning of OCD. It is also important that your psychologist is experienced in treating kids who have OCD. This is not always easy to determine. When Dr. M and I first saw my psychologist, who was recommended by my psychiatrist, we asked him if he saw many patients who have OCD, and he reassured us that he did. In time, however, we were to discover that his methods for dealing with OCD were incomplete. Not wrong, just incomplete.

I spent several sessions with my psychologist talking about how my OCD thoughts were not based on any reality. I was asked to challenge the logistical aspects of my thoughts and to try to resist my compulsions. The experts call this approach cognitive behavioral therapy, and it apparently works very well for mild OCD and for those who have other mental disorders, such as depression and anxiety. It did help me some; I slowly improved over the two months of my weekly therapy sessions. After the two months, however, my progress slowed and then stalled. I didn't get worse, but I didn't get any better, and I still had plenty of OCD symptoms. In other words, I still had a long way to go and it seemed, at least to me, that my psychologist was out of ideas. In fact, during my last two sessions with him, we hadn't talked about anything new or made any new plans to deal with my OCD. He even suggested that we decrease the frequency of our sessions to every other week instead of every week. Personally, I was fine with this plan. I didn't really like the sessions and talking about my OCD, but Dr. M thought differently. She knew I needed more help, not less.

We made the mistake of not asking specific questions about how my psychologist planned to treat my OCD. The therapy that most experts on OCD currently recommend is called exposure and response (or ritual) prevention therapy (ERP). This therapy, which I was to eventually undertake, consists essentially of facing your fears and then resisting doing your compulsions. It is very different, and much, much, much, harder than just talking about your OCD. ERP requires you to actively confront your OCD and to not back down. ERP is what you need to do if you want to beat your OCD.

The bottom line is this: You will need the help of a psychologist (or other mental health professional). Be sure, however, that the one you pick is well versed in ERP and is willing to push you into actually doing the ERP. How to do this? Have your parents ask lots of questions before they agree to an actual visit. Read up on ERP and on how it's done, so that you and your parents know the right questions to ask. Also, check out the OCD Foundation website, because on that site is listed qualified psychologists. I know that these recommendations aren't easy to do. If you are suffering, you want immediate help. You don't want to wait while the adults around you sort out the necessary information and make a decision. But, try to be patient. You need, and deserve, the right help.

What is exposure and response prevention therapy?

Exposure and response prevention therapy (ERP) is exactly what its name says. You expose yourself to what you fear and try to prevent the response that you use to decrease those fears. In a way, ERP prevents you from running away from your fears. It works for OCD, because it makes you challenge what you fear. Once you see that your fears are not real, but are a trick of OCD, you will be amazed at how fast those fears disappear. You can then realize that your OCD thoughts are not absolutely awful and that you are now empowered to overcome those thoughts.

I used ERP and was shocked at how fast I got better. Of course, it doesn't work overnight, but if you persistently work at it, you will succeed. One of the tricks for making ERP work is to start simple. Don't try to take on your most difficult fear at the beginning. Think about all your OCD obsessions and compulsions, and I'm sure you will recognize that some are more intense and cause you more distress than others. Find the easiest ones and start there. Once you have some success at the first levels, you then need to doggedly work your way to the hardest ones.

The main problem with ERP is how hard it is to get started. I actually thought that Dr. M was crazy when she told me what I needed to do with ERP. I had spent a long time trying to avoid my obsessions and doing my compulsions to make me feel better, that I couldn't imagine how I was to actually confront those thoughts. This whole process of ERP seemed way too scary and impossible for me to accomplish. How was I to start? What could Dr. M possibly do that would help me approach ERP? The answer turned out to be embarrassingly simple and self-centered on my part. She paid me.

Right before one Christmas break, Dr. M told me about ERP and how she thought it was the key for me to get over OCD. Of course, I balked. I wanted nothing to do with it until she told me the specifics. We were to have multiple sessions on OCD over a two-week period. During that time, we would work on OCD. We would talk about OCD, read book passages on OCD, and directly expose me to words and images that had sexual content. And, to get me through this "torture," Dr. M. would give me $1,000. I have to admit that it was the reward and not the actual prospect of getting over OCD that helped me approach ERP. I realize that not all parents can afford to give a lot of money, but I bet that in many cases some kind of a deal can be worked out. You need motivation to do ERP. It is hard work, and you will hate it. You will want to quit and go back to your OCD even though it keeps you down. For me, a reward got me started and kept me going.

How does exposure and response prevention therapy work?

Before treatment, most people who have OCD, including me, deal with their obsessive thoughts by repressing those thoughts (or at least, trying to). Whenever they are experiencing a serious bout of thoughts, they try to avoid those obsessions in any way possible. Why confront the monster when you can just run around it? They might, for example, go to sleep, distract themselves by watching TV, or in my case, play a video game. Adults sometimes throw themselves into their work and become workaholics or students sometimes become so involved in their schoolwork that it becomes another obsession. Doesn't sound so bad, does it? Maybe it even it helps some OCDers become successful. But, what happens when the work or the fun stops, or when we wake up? The obsessions come roaring back, and sometimes, they are even more powerful.

ERP takes away your habit of thought repression and makes you confront your thoughts. It works by making you develop new habits for dealing with your obsessions. In fact, some OCD experts have proven that after doing ERP, the brains of those who have OCD actually change and look more normal. In a way, ERP fixes the broken brain circuits and allows for healthy ones to take over. I just wish someone would develop an easier and less painful way to accomplish this. I would have happily undergone anything, even brain surgery, if it meant I could have avoided doing ERP.

Another way to think about ERP is that it embraces the pain of the obsessions, which takes away their power. Thoughts that don't cause pain become just thoughts; they are no longer obsessions. Yet another way to think about it is that ERP makes you less sensitive to your obsessions. It's like jumping into a swimming pool of cool water. You know it's going to be cold, and you hesitate before you jump. Some people may even get too afraid of the cold water and decide not to jump. Those who jump in, however, and deal with the initial cold soon get used to the water, and it eventually feels warmer. Their bodies have gotten used to the cold because they have become desensitized or habituated to it. ERP works in the same way. Don't take my word for it, however, jump in and see for yourself.

Before ERP can work for you, you have to take on the pain of your obsessions. In fact, you will probably even feel worse for a while before you notice any benefits of ERP. Let me assure you, however, that it's worth it. Through ERP, your obsessions will lose their power and soon you will even wonder why these thoughts originally bothered you. But, for

ERP to work, you have to make a commitment to it. There is no other way to take the power from OCD except by directly confronting it. Even though it sounds tempting to just keep running away from OCD, keep in mind that those who are always running are also tired from that running. Why not just invest most of your energy at once in ERP so that you can enjoy the rest of your life?

I also think of ERP as my most effective weapon in my arsenal against OCD. Once I learned how to use this weapon, I knew that OCD would never again take over my life. Whenever I sense that OCD is stalking me and waiting to pounce, I just whip out my weapon, fire it up, and watch OCD run away. ERP doesn't completely kill off OCD. But, it sure does come close.

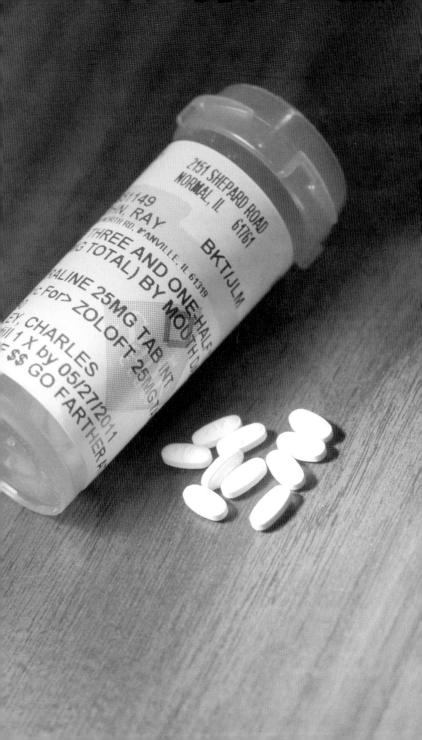

WHAT DID YOU DO DURING YOUR FIRST SESSION OF EXPOSURE AND RESPONSE PREVENTION THERAPY?

The best way to start ERP and the one that will cause the least pain to your family is to have your psychologist or other mental health professional help you. The first steps should consist of you and your psychologist making a list of all your obsessions and their associated compulsions. Then, you should order those obsessions from the least bothersome to the most painful. For example, for me, touching a doorknob that I thought was contaminated was multitudes less stressful than thinking about touching my penis in a sexual way. Your psychologist may even have you rate each obsession/compulsion combination on some sort of anxiety scale. The next step is to make a plan on how to tackle those items on your list. What timetable are you going to use? Who is going to keep you honest about what you do? And, most importantly, how are you going to get started? Chances are that just making the list will cause you a lot of distress. The last thing you want to do is to actually face what's on that list. But, if you want to beat OCD, you need to start. Like many other things in life, start at the bottom and work your way up.

My OCD symptoms were no longer at their worst when I started using ERP. I had been on medication for a while, and I had tried to change my thinking patterns to ways that were less accommodating to my OCD. But, OCD was still very much a part of me. Dr. M was also worried because my progress towards getting better had slowed. By this time, she had read many books on OCD, had done research about ERP, and was convinced that this was the way to go. The problem was: How to get started? We considered several options: 1) Go back to our psychologist and insist that he use ERP with me, 2) Find a different psychologist who is more familiar with ERP, or 3) Try it by ourselves. We quickly dismissed the first two options. Neither one of us really wanted to go back to my psychologist. He was kind and caring to us, and he really did try to help me, but Dr. M didn't think he knew enough about ERP. We also didn't want to waste any more time working with someone who is just learning a new technique. The other problem we had stems from where we live. Our community is relatively small and because of that, there aren't many choices with regards to mental health professionals. To find someone with the needed expertise on ERP, we would have to travel quite a distance. Of course, Dr. M was willing to do this if necessary, but again, we figured that this approach would take too long. This left the third option of trying it ourselves.

Doing ERP without outside help is definitely not for everyone, but it worked for me and Dr. M. It helped that she was a physician and was used to talking with patients and their parents about mental health issues. The downside, of course, was that she is my mom and not my doctor. The roles that she took on to implement my ERP plan were many and sometimes confusing. She was my coach who yelled instructions and encouragement from the sidelines; she was a taskmaster who pushed and then pushed me some more; she was my teacher who explained the steps we needed to take; and of course, she was my mother, who comforted me when I fell apart. Were there times when Dr. M screwed up her roles? Sure, especially in the beginning there were times when I needed her to back off, and she didn't. She knew the harder we pushed, the faster I would get better. But, I couldn't always move as fast as she thought I could. During these times, we would end up yelling at each other and thinking about how we should give up and find help. Inevitably though, Dr. M would wipe her tears, I would stop my raging, and we would try again. It was hard to see at the time, but each instance when we messed up and fell down, we learned something. In time and with a lot of practice, we got better and our times of difficulty became fewer and further between.

To start off my first ERP session, we read out loud from textbooks on human sexuality. Dr. M had found several of these textbooks that had been used in a nearby university for a course on human sexuality. At first, she let me choose what paragraphs to read. Of course, I chose the ones that didn't bother me at all. You would think that in a book on sex that I would have trouble finding paragraphs that didn't trigger my obsessions, but you would be wrong. Somehow, I found those passages very quickly. Dr. M, however, would always choose the topics that bothered me. At times, I wondered if she did it just to make me mad, but then I would remember what ERP was supposed to do: challenge me. I had to listen to Dr. M read paragraphs on masturbation, sexual desire, sexual positions, and just about everything else to do with sex. Most males my age would find pleasure in reading this information (not if their mother were reading it to them, of course). But, for me it was hard. With the mention of any word dealing with sex (eg, penis, vagina, breasts, intercourse, masturbation) I could feel my body tense throughout, my heart rate increase, my breathing become shallower, and I would feel an intense urge to wash my hands. I could also feel anger bubbling up in me, and it was hard not to throw down the books and run away. Then, like magic, it got a little better. With each reading, I didn't feel as bad. I still felt bad, but not as intense as it was when we first started. This is one of the most important keys to doing ERP: Stay with it until you feel your symptoms decreasing.

Once I had survived this first round of ERP, Dr. M stepped it up a little. This is another important aspect of ERP: Don't get in a hurry. Small steps are OK. Just be sure to keep moving. For the second round, she insisted that I (and not just her) read out loud from the difficult paragraphs. The difference here was that I had to say the words and not just hear them when Dr. M read out loud. Again, I hated it, felt angry, and wanted very badly to wash my hands. And, again, it got slowly got better with each reading. Next, Dr. M insisted that I actually look at the pictures in the books. I remember having to hold down my anxiety as I looked at the many, different possible sexual positions that two people could use to have sex. Even though the pictures were drawings and not actual photographs, I still found them almost impossible to look at. Throughout all this, Dr. M was close by, encouraging me, trying not to yell back when I yelled at her, and most importantly, making sure that I didn't cheat. And, I tried very hard to cheat. I thought that if I didn't look directly at the pictures, but at the words underneath the pictures or at something on the picture, like a foot, then I wouldn't have to face my fears by looking at the other "parts." But, Dr. M had been ready for this possibility, and she always watched my eyes to see exactly where I was looking. Most times, she caught me and reminded me about how it was necessary to do the hard work if I wanted to get over OCD.

For two weeks straight we worked on ERP. It was over Christmas vacation so I didn't have to worry about schoolwork or grades. Each day, we would start out by doing whatever activity I had mastered the day before (like reading out loud from the textbooks). That way, I could remind myself of the progress I was making. Then, I would have to try something new (like looking at the pictures) that was as hard or even harder than what I did the day before. We had to take frequent breaks so that I could blow off steam by playing video games or watching TV. We also usually tried to do the most difficult activities in the morning and leave the less intense ones for the evening. On most evenings, Dr. M and I would watch television programs or movies that had varying degrees of sexual content. In the beginning, I had problems even watching programs like *Family Guy*. In fact, there were times when I would feel anxious every time a woman or girl appeared on the screen. I would often yell "bad thought" as my compulsion during these times and ask Dr. M if I could wash my hands. Eventually though, I found that I could watch more and more without feeling as much anxiety.

Also, during this time, we worked on some annoying habits that OCD had instilled in me. For example, I had yet to become comfortable touching all doorknobs in our home and would often use something, like a piece of paper or a napkin, as a barrier between my hand and the doorknob. Or, I would insist that someone else open it for me. Many times I could even coerce Dr. M into opening a door for me. All I had to do was to wait when she was really busy with something else and then pitch a fit about the door. I would yell something like, "I need to study because I have a real hard test tomorrow. You are stressing me out, and if you don't open the door, I won't be able to concentrate on studying. You're messing me up. Do you want me to fail my test?" She would sigh because she knew that OCD had enforced its will yet once again. Then, she would open the door to shut me up so she could back to what she had been working on. Obviously, this OCD-directed behavior, and many others, needed to stop.

I was relieved to finally get to the end of those two weeks and get back to something easy like school. When I looked back, however, I was shocked at how much I had accomplished. Even more incredible to me was how much better I was feeling. My anxiety level had markedly decreased, and I could do things now that I couldn't have before doing the ERP. I could now watch certain television programs, and I could even watch sexual scenes in movies without begging to fast forward through them. What did Dr. M notice? She noticed the same as I did, of course, but also something else. Before the ERP, Dr. M told me that when we were out in public, I would always get nervous right after I walked past a woman or girl and then beg to leave wherever we were because of my rapidly increasing anxiety. I don't remember this, but right before school was to restart for the new year, we went shopping at a grocery store. I walked in, walked around, and spent a lot of time calmly looking at different things. To anyone else this was ordinary behavior. To Dr. M, however, it was incredible, because I never once said anything about wanting to leave or about how many bad thoughts I was having. Never during my ERP sessions had this particular behavior been targeted, but now it was gone. Dr. M and I were now officially believers in ERP.

How many exposure and response prevention therapy sessions will I have to do before my OCD is gone?

It is impossible to predict how many and how often you will need to have ERP sessions. If you are working with a psychologist, then you might have weekly sessions that are one to two hours long or you may be given ERP homework to do at home with your parents. Also factoring in is the severity of your OCD and your motivation to get better. I suggest that you have as many ERP sessions as you can stand and as quickly as you can have them. Don't lose any more of your life to OCD than what you absolutely have to.

What worked for Dr. M and I was to have my ERP sessions during school breaks. We were afraid that if I tried to do too much OCD work at the same time school was happening, then my grades would plummet, and I would have a whole new set of problems. In total, we did about five of these sessions, spread over about one year. The shortest time duration for my sessions was one week, usually spring break, and the longest was never over two weeks. We found that our stamina for doing this kind of therapy would only last about two weeks. After that, neither one of us was functioning well, and it wasn't worth the effort to even try.

For me, no two ERP sessions were the same. For each one, Dr. M would have a general set of goals for us to accomplish that she would then refine depending on how the session was progressing or not. She picked out each set of goals by watching and listening to me between our sessions. She would take note of what OCD symptoms I was continuing to have and think about how we could target those symptoms through ERP. Sometimes, the symptoms were very specific. For example, for a long time I would never eat anything, like a potato chip or a French fry, that had fallen anywhere on my lap. My OCD brain would scream at me telling me that the food item was contaminated by semen that had found its way to the outside of my pants. Of course, I would insist that the food item be thrown out. I wouldn't even let my cats eat anything that had fallen on my pants. To deal with this symptom, we purposely dropped pieces of food on my lap. Of course, we had to start at about my knee and then gradually, work closer to my genital area. What did we do with the food after it was dropped? We ate it. At first, I wouldn't let Dr. M eat the food, but as the session progressed, I did. By the end of the ERP session, I didn't feel any further anxiety about food, or any other item, that I might accidently drop onto my lap. I know this was ridiculous, but think of all the times you drop stuff, and its hits your lap. Then, try to imagine that you panic every time this happens and insist on throwing out or washing whatever it was that fell. Now do you understand just how much of a victory this was for me?

During other parts of my multiple ERP sessions, we would work on obsessions that were more generalized than the one about items falling on my lap. For a long time, I continued to experience bad thoughts about women or girls and needed either to wash my hands or to confess to Dr. M about my thoughts before I would feel less panicked. At one time, just about any female that I would see, any picture of any female that I happened to see, or anytime a sexual thought popped into my brain made me anxious. In short, I was a mess. Just think about the number of times one sees or encounters females in a day's time. Also, I am a teenage male; guess how often sexual comments are made by my friends. I was surrounded by the one thing I feared the most. I knew that if OCD was to become a lesser part of my life, I needed to conquer my sexual obsessions. Dr. M knew it too and always made this a goal in our sessions.

I had to complete, or from my perspective survive, several ERP activities that specifically targeted sexual obsessions, before I finally concluded that maybe OCD would let me be. We did these activities at different times spread throughout our ERP sessions. They were intense and difficult, not only for me but also for Dr. M. I know that she would have felt more confident about our ERP sessions if she could have followed some sort of manual or guideline about how to deal with sexual obsessions. But, no such information could be found, and we were left to figure it out on our own. Much of what we did took courage on Dr. M's part, because some of our ERP activities were borderline weird. I have often wondered what would have happened if anyone walked in and saw what we were doing. Until now, we have never told anyone else about our ERP sessions because of the sensitive nature of their main focus (ie, sex). Many times I debated about whether or not to include some of this information in this book, but finally, I decided it was important. What we did worked, and if we truly want to help our fellow OCDers, then we have to show how we did it. So, what exactly did we do?

- Looked repeatedly at a *Playboy* magazine. Dr. M and I did this over several ERP sessions. Page by page, Dr. M would go through the magazine with me and made sure that I actually looked at the pictures. To help lessen any embarrassment that I would obviously feel, we actually started out looking at a *Playgirl* magazine. Dr. M said that it was only fair that if I was expected to do something this weird that she should to. This was something I appreciated. It was like she was also putting her dignity on the line to help me.

- Watched sexually explicit scenes in movies. Dr. M would find such a scene and make me watch it over and over again. At first, we watched scenes that were more suggestive than explicit. Then, we watched more intense scenes. We didn't go as far as to watch pornography (Dr. M considered it and would have used it if necessary). But, we found some movies that were close (eg, had scenes with male and female nudity and actual sexual intercourse).

- Once I could get through looking at *Playboy* without feeling like I was going to explode, Dr. M had me look at pictures in another pornographic magazine (*Hustler*). This magazine has more sexually explicit pictures than *Playboy* and even now, I am still shocked that Dr. M did this. I know she didn't condone what she saw, but we bulled through it anyway.

- Wrote out and recorded short vignettes that had a sexual and personal storyline. Dr. M had read in several books on OCD that by saying out loud and recording what you fear the most, you can lessen that fear. The trick is to listen repeatedly to the recording until you actually become bored by it. Also, it is important that no reassuring wording is included. Words like "even though I would never do that" or "I know that this is only my OCD" only serve to lessen the impact of your recording. We did several of these recordings. Sometimes, I wrote the scenarios and on other times, Dr. M did. It was important, however, that I do all the recordings, because for this to work, I had to hear my voice say the words and describe the actions. We started out with a short scenario and once I could tolerate listening to that one, I moved on to longer and more intense ones. Here is some of what I recorded.

Recording # 1

I was walking through Walmart when I saw a pretty girl who appeared to be about 16. She was wearing very short shorts and wore a revealing shirt. I could see part of her breasts. I had an erection. I could feel something wet in my pants. In the bathroom, I saw wet semen in my pants.

Recording #2

I was walking through Walmart, and I saw a girl. She was wearing a shirt revealing her breasts. I could see she was wearing a black, lacy bra. She was also wearing short shorts and had a very sexy butt. I think she was the sexiest woman I had ever seen. I got an erection when I looked at her. Later, when I was taking a shower, I thought about the sexy lady, I got another erection, and I masturbated. The semen washed away down the drain, and I felt happy.

Recording #3

I was at a party with some friends, and they were watching a pornographic movie. I stopped to watch for a long time. I watched a man and a woman having sex, and they were really going at it. The woman was on top of the man, and she was moving up and down. Her breasts were very big, and they were bouncing all around. They were both groaning and making a lot of noise. After a few minutes of this, they both had orgasms. Then, the movie showed another man and woman having sex. This time the man was behind the woman and was moving back and forth. The man ejaculated, and then fell over the woman's back. Then, the movie showed another couple. This time the woman was giving the man oral sex. Her mouth was moving up and down the man's penis, and he was groaning. When he ejaculated, his sperm got all over the woman's mouth. When I was watching this movie, I got an erection, and all my friends also got erections. I know this because we were all joking about it when we were going home. When I got home, I went into the downstairs bathroom to take a shower. I was thinking about the movie and all the naked women that I had seen. I got a big erection and masturbated while thinking about those women. My ejaculation was so intense that I got some of it on the shower wall.

Dr. M had considered several other storylines, but decided that I had progressed far enough with the ones we did. On such storyline dealt with my obsession of fearing that I would somehow sexually molest someone, especially someone much younger than me. Fortunately, this particular fear melted away with the other ones after writing and recording the other scenarios. I know, however, that Dr. M would have had me write a scenario in which I had sexually molested a child if she thought it would have helped me deal with my OCD. To many, I realize that this idea sounds repulsive and perhaps even pathological, but this is what we OCDers might have to do. That is, if we want to get better.

The recordings, like everything else to do with ERP, were hard to do, but they proved to be an effective tool against OCD. Dr. M remembers that during the writing and recording of the first one (the easiest) I had started having eye and shoulder tics. I had never had any previous problems with tics, but the intensity of the recordings somehow brought it out. By the end of all the recordings, however, the tics had stopped.

WASN'T IT STRANGE TO TALK TO YOUR MOM ABOUT YOUR SEXUAL OBSESSIONS?

For many of us who have OCD, it will be our psychologists and not our parents who are the ones we talk to the most about our obsessions. In my case, however, it was Dr. M and yes, talking to my mother about sexual matters was weird. It often added to my stress when I had to talk to my mother about my explicit sexual obsessions. Although Dr. M is a pediatrician and has a lot of experience talking with parents and children, I found it hard to give her the full attention and respect a psychologist deserved. I think this was because of the natural relationship that exists between teenagers and their mothers. It is important for us teenagers to break away from our parents and to accomplish this, we often argue with them and refuse to listen to their opinions.

Dr. M was fully aware of the difficulties I had talking with her about my sexual obsessions. To help me, she tried separating her mother role from her doctor role. She had me refer to her as Dr. St. John, and she talked to me like she would any other patient. We found that this separation of identities helped me talk to her about my obsessions. It was like I was no longer talking to my mother about sex but a doctor who was trained to handle such matters.

But, even though this separation helped, it still wasn't quite right. In my experience, doctors are often too distant and uninvolved in our lives to really help in situations like mine. So, when Dr. M assumed her doctor role, I had a hard time believing that my doctor was really going to help me. It was like we needed an intermediary between my doctor and my mother. I needed someone I was comfortable talking to about my sexual obsessions but who also knew me, loved me, and would fight for me. We found this someone in Hank: a character we purposely developed to help me fight my OCD.

Describing who Hank is and how he fits into my OCD therapy is not easy. In fact, whenever I try to talk to others about Hank, I always make him sound hokey and implausible. But, I'll try, because I think that it's important for you to understand Hank and how he helped me. Hank is like a spiritual guide in that he doesn't exist in a real form that we can all see and touch. He does, however, have a voice and speaks through Dr. M. In our minds, he takes the form of one of our most beloved cats. For many years, we have had many cats in our home, and Hank was the most calm and loving of them all. He would often sit with me while Dr. M and I had our ERP sessions and would comfort me during times of stress. Eventually, Dr. M found a way for Hank to speak during our sessions, and I found that I could listen to him easier than I could to Dr. M.

One reason that I think Hank worked out so well was because he never lost his patience with me. Whenever Dr. M would get intense during my ERP sessions, I would ask for Hank, and he would appear at the same time that Dr. M would disappear. He could calm me in ways that no one else could and convince me to continue with my ERP session. Even though I knew that it was really Dr. M directing what Hank said, somehow I could focus on Hank and not on Dr. M. I know that this sounds silly, but it worked for us because I could always listen to Hank. He became a fundamental part of my journey to being OCD free. I don't know if finding a character like Hank is possible for everyone who has OCD. But, I know that I wouldn't have made it without his help.

How do I know if I'm doing the exposure and response prevention therapy right?

Doing ERP is like many other things in life: no pain, no gain. Many times, you will want to quit because of how much it hurts. And, you wouldn't be alone. Some books on OCD mention that close to ¼ of us who try ERP don't succeed with it because we can't take the pain and give up. I also think that ERP fails with some of us because we don't push ourselves hard enough. In other words, we take on some pain, but not nearly enough. To me, doing ERP felt like I was training for a marathon.

The easiest way to know if you are doing ERP right is by asking yourself one simple question: Is my OCD getting any better? If your obsessions are becoming less bothersome, and if you are doing less of your compulsions, then you know that you are on the right track. But, like everything else to do with OCD, there is a trick. When you first start with ERP, it might actually make you worse before you get better. Chances are your anxiety levels will increase when you first face your fears. Even thinking about challenging your obsessions can make those obsessions more intense. But, you need to understand that this uptick in anxiousness won't last very long and that with a little more time and effort, your anxiety will decrease. And then, if you really stay with ERP, your anxiety might even dwindle down to almost nothing.

Dr. M says she often knew that we were on the right track with ERP when she saw me get angry or agitated. If I had been sitting before starting our ERP, I would often get up and pace if she suggested an activity I knew would be hard. At times, I would leave the room for a minute to calm myself down. There was even a short time when I had tics (eye blinking and shoulder shrugging) every time I challenged my OCD. I think that if I had ever readily agreed to do an ERP activity, that Dr. M would have changed her mind about that activity right away.

To help gauge how hard an ERP activity is, some therapists use a scale. Most use a scale of one to ten with one being no anxiety and ten the most extreme anxiety you have ever felt. A good ERP activity would be one that you rate high (at least eight or higher). The same scale is also often used to help determine when ERP is working. If, for example, you initially rated an activity as a ten but then later, rated that same activity as a five, then you know you were successful. Sometimes, the scale is even used to help determine how long an activity needs to be. Your therapist might ask you throughout an activity to rate your anxiety, and when your rating has substantially decreased, then stop that activity. One time that I specifically remember when Dr. M and I used this scale was when I needed to deal with my anxiety about a certain bathroom in our house. I had often masturbated in this bathroom at a time when my OCD had yet to get a hold of me. My OCD had convinced me that anyone or anything that had ever used that bathroom or had even walked into that bathroom was now contaminated with my semen. We had even dubbed this bathroom, "the evil bathroom." This thinking, of course, is ludicrous but that's what OCD does to you. To help me get over this obsession, Dr. M first had me step just over the threshold of the bathroom door and stand there. At first, my anxiety was close to a ten, but then as I stood there, my anxiety decreased, and when I felt it was close to a five, Dr. M let me step back out. We did variations of this activity, and each time we used the scale to determine when we could move on. In time, I progressed from just standing in the bathroom to actually taking a shower in that bathroom. Now, I just walk in and use it without feeling any anxiety at all.

Many times when doing my ERP, I was tempted to cheat and say that certain activities weren't as hard as they really were or to find ways not to fully engage with those activities. Sometimes I did cheat, but mostly I didn't, because Dr. M was always watching and found ways to keep me honest. With each successful round of ERP I was feeling less anxious and more like who I used to be. ERP was working, and I realized that the harder I worked at it, the faster I was getting better. There even came a time during some of my last ERP activities that I was on my honor to complete them. Dr. M knew that I had to become more comfortable with my body and to accomplish this, she suggested that I spend some time looking at my naked self and become more comfortable with touching my body. For obvious reasons, she couldn't chaperone these particular activities. I was on my own. It was time for me to fly solo. Did I cheat and then lie to Dr. M about it? What do you think?

I UNDERSTAND THAT I NEED TO DO EXPO-SURE AND RESPONSE PREVENTION THERAPY, BUT WHAT ELSE CAN I DO TO HELP ME GET OVER OCD?

Exposure and response prevention therapy is the key to defeating OCD, but there are also many smaller things you can do to make the fight easier. If you really want to win against OCD, you need to muster all the strength you can and to do this, you need to find what helps you the most.

I found that getting adequate sleep, managing my daily stress, and keeping up my health through diet and exercise were three things that helped me the most. I discovered that if I could put each of these three factors in a good place, then my fight against OCD was that much simpler. If, for example, I stayed up late but couldn't sleep in the next day, I often had a hard time dealing with my OCD. It was like the necessary energy I needed to fight against OCD had been depleted. And, it is hard to deal with something as complicated as OCD when you're feeling groggy. Getting enough sleep, however, proved to be difficult at times. Sometimes my OCD thoughts kept me awake, and sometimes I just couldn't go to sleep for reasons unknown. To help me fall asleep, I would often watch a movie that I was very familiar with (I think I have watched *Shawshank Redemption* at least one hundred and fifty times). By doing this, I could concentrate on something but could still allow myself to relax. At other times when I knew I really needed sleep, I would take an over-the-counter medication called melatonin. Melatonin is a hormone we all have in our brains, and its job is to help us regulate our sleep-wake cycles. Melatonin helps me get to sleep, and I often feel good the next day. If you decide that you want to try melatonin to help regulate your sleep, I would suggest that you ask a physician about it or do some reading on it. For melatonin to work well, you need to find the best dose for you and to find the best time of the evening to take it. Dr. M and I have had to experiment with both doses and timing before we found the best way to use melatonin.

Improving my physical health has also helped me deal with OCD. After my OCD had gotten better, I started working on improving my physical fitness. I couldn't start right away because my OCD was just too intense, and I couldn't focus on anything else other than trying to beat back OCD and going to school. Once I got better, I took up running and weightlifting and continue these activities to this day. I found that as I progressed, I felt better both physically and mentally. Even though I know that my mental improvement was mainly because of the ERP we were doing, I think that the exercise also helped.

And, I am definitely not the only one whose mental disorder was helped by exercise. Dr. M has found several studies which show that exercise improves the functioning of those who have a mental illness, such as depression. There was even a study showing how exercise improves brain function by increasing the amounts of certain hormones that are needed to rebuild brain cells (neurons) and their connections with each other. It is hard to know for sure, but I think that exercise was one reason why I did so well and was able stop taking my OCD medication.

I also combined exercise with improving my diet. Prior to this time, I ate whatever I wanted, which was mainly fast food and processed foods. I was never overweight, but I realize now that I couldn't have been getting all the nutrition I needed. In time, I have changed my eating habits to include more fruits and vegetables and have definitely decreased the amount of fast food I eat. I don't know if these changes have helped my OCD or not, but they certainly didn't hurt.

Another thing that helped me deal with OCD was to decrease any unnecessary stress in my life. Note that I didn't say all stress, just the stress that doesn't help. In fact, we all need some stress to keep us going. Would any of us ever study if we didn't have tests or grades to worry about? Would we practice if we didn't have a performance to think about? I think that to have a fulfilling and complete life is one where good stress has played a part. Bad stress, however, causes us OCDers to have more symptoms. When we're stressed out, you can bet that our symptoms will flare and in some cases, get completely out of control. Dr. M and I have worked on decreasing my stress levels by trying to keep me organized both at home and at school, by decreasing the intensity of our home environment, and by letting me blow off stream when I need to. Whenever I feel as if I'm going to blow, I watch movies, play video games, go for a walk, or lift some weights. The important thing is to have a short time period where you can forget about your trials and tribulations.

WHAT MISTAKES DID YOU MAKE WHEN DEALING WITH YOUR OCD?

My main mistakes were not having enough motivation in the beginning to take on OCD and not having enough courage to push through with treatment once we got started. Dr. M's mistakes centered mainly on pushing me too hard during treatment and getting impatient with me when I hesitated to do certain therapies. I would often protest to further treatment after my limit had been reached, but Dr. M, thinking that the more pain, the more gain, would attempt to enforce more therapy. She failed to realize that treating OCD is like muscle building, you need to recover between exercise sessions if you want to get stronger.

Dr. M also made the mistake of sometimes getting in my way when I needed to do a compulsion. There were times, for example, when she would physically stand between me and the sink where I washed my hands. As hard as I tried, there were instances when OCD got the best of me and would force me to wash my hands. During these times, there was no stopping me, and I would push anything or anyone out of my way. I remember one time when I actually pushed Dr. M hard enough that she fell down. I had become extremely upset about my bedding, thinking that it was contaminated and insisting that it be washed. I was holding my sheets and blankets and was about to run for the washing machine when Dr. M tried to stop me. My anxiety was so strong, and my OCD was so out of control that I knocked her down when she tried to stop me.

Dr. M freely admits that she pushed too hard at times. She says it's partly because she hated my OCD so much and what it was doing to me. She also wanted to go on with her own life but didn't think she could until I was safe from OCD. She wishes that she had used more patience and calmness when dealing with me. We both understand now that taking small, but sure steps works better than trying to take larger and more reckless ones.

When I think back, I wished that I had learned quicker to stand up to OCD. If I had garnered the necessary courage and motivation earlier, then I wouldn't have suffered so much and would be further along in my life. I think that it took me so long to begin my fight because I didn't fully understand what OCD was and how much damage it was doing. In the beginning, I actually thought that I would rather live my life with OCD rather than without it. To think that a person would rather live with a mental illness seems absurd, but this is the power of OCD. I thought that without OCD that I wouldn't recognize the evil in me, and that the only way I would protect others from that evil was to embrace my OCD. In my OCD-twisted mind all my confessing, hand/feet washing, showering, and clothes washing were done to protect others. It was only when I understood how OCD had tricked me into this weird thinking that I finally got angry enough to fight back.

End of My Story — For Now

Today, I am OCD free. No one gave me this freedom from OCD; I worked hard to attain it. Even though my OCD appears gone, I know that it still lurks in me, ready to strike if I ever decrease my vigilance. OCD can be beaten, buried, and almost forgotten, but it can't be killed. It will always be a part of me, but I am determined to keep that part as small as possible. I plan never again to let OCD dictate to me where I go, what I do, or what my future holds.

OCD tried hard to take my life away and on several occasions, it came close. There were times when both Dr. M and I got tired and seriously considered quitting. But, we also knew that quitting would mean a victory for OCD and a compromised life for me. Somehow, we always rallied and found the strength to fight on.

There is no doubt that OCD has scarred me and that I will forever carry those scars. It would be naïve of me to think that I could go through something as intense as OCD and not have it leave its mark. But, I'm not ashamed of these scars. In fact, if I could, I would show off my OCD battle scars because I am proud of what I have done. If it were up to me, I would have all of us OCDers, who have managed to beat back our OCD, wear a distinguishing badge that tells the world around us who we are and what we have done. What we have accomplished deserves honor and recognition. We have stood our ground and faced our fears. How many people can really claim such a victory?

I hope that after reading this book, you are now a little stronger and have more hope about your future. I know that with time, patience, and perseverance you will take back your life from OCD. I did. The journey was long and many times, I wanted to quit. But, I kept going, and now that I'm on the other side of OCD, I can tell you that every step and every painful moment was worth it. We all deserve a great life. Don't let OCD get in your way.

Acknowledgments

I would like to thank my father, H. Tak Cheung, for using his expertise in text design and photography in the production of this book.

I also need to thank my mother, Joni St. John (a.k.a. Dr. M) for her editing skills and for her belief that I had something important to say.

Photo Annotations

Page 6. This photo was taken inside the subway with my grandpa during our visit to Hong Kong to see my paternal grandmother. I was very close to my grandpa until my OCD started to control my life. He died two months before the completion of this book, but I know he would have been very proud of me. I have dedicated this book to his memory.

Page 12. This photo was on my eighth birthday with my mom's homemade chocolate cake. My OCD symptoms already started to surface by this time.

Page 46. This photo was taken along the bank of the Vermilion River that is near to our house. It is a beautiful place, and we have taken many walks up and down the river in sunshine, rain, and snow.

Page 68. I was standing on top of the grain wagon during the fall harvest in this photo, which was taken shortly before we moved to Shanghai, China.

Page 74. This photo was taken at an afterschool basketball program in the elementary school that I attended during my year in Shanghai.

I did not speak Mandarin Chinese when I first arrived, but by the time when we left, I could carry out simple conversations.

Page 86.   Shortly after returning home from China, my OCD started to take a downward turn, and I had an increasing frequency of obtrusive sexual thoughts.

Page 92.   The exposure and response prevention therapy was wearing me down. This photo shows the despondency on my face during my junior year in high school.

Page 104.   This photo was taken in one of the canyons at the Starved Rock State Park, located 45 miles from our house. I enjoy walking through the canyons when it is quiet with no other visitors. It is my favorite place, and it offers me an escape in my worst OCD moments.

Page 114. This is the photo of Hank and me. Through his voice, I was able to address some of the most difficult issues concerning my OCD.

Page 122.   Cats have been an important part in my fight against OCD. They have never failed to give affection, especially when I need it most.

Page 128. For over two years, a SSRI has been my daily companion. I know that medication helped me some, but I was glad to finally get off. Since August 2010, I have not needed any further medication.

Page 148. This photo was taken during my sophomore year in high school as I was charging my father with a sword. This was about the time when my mother and I decided to try exposure and response prevention therapy. This photo symbolizes my resolution to defeat OCD.

Page 160. This photo was taken as I sat next to my mom along the river bank by our house on a beautiful fall day. I had begun my road to recovery through sessions of exposure and response and prevention therapy.

Page 164. This photo was taken with my mom on the northern California coast during our trip to the Redwood National Park.

Page 166. This photo was taken in the summer of 2010 as we were riding on a tram in Hong Kong. By this time, I had almost fully recovered and was enjoying life.

Front and back cover photos. These photos were taken at the Peak, the highest point on the Hong Kong Island in the summer of 2010. A rain cloud had just passed over the peak, revealing the distant sunlight. These photos symbolize the hope for me in winning the battle against OCD.

All photographs were taken by my father H. Tak Cheung.